Knowledge Management Strategies

Jerry Honeycutt

PUBLISHED BY
Microsoft Press
A Division of Microsoft Corporation
One Microsoft Way
Redmond, Washington 98052-6399

Library of Congress Cataloging-in-Publication Data
Honeycutt, Jerry.
    Knowledge Management Strategies / Jerry Honeycutt.
        p. cm.
    ISBN 0-7356-0724-9
    1. Knowledge management.   I. Title.
    HD30.2 .H66   2000
    658.4'038--dc21   00-035158

Printed and bound in the United States of America.

1 2 3 4 5 6 7 8 9   WCWC   5 4 3 2 1 0

Distributed in Canada by Penguin Books Canada Limited.

A CIP catalogue record for this book is available from the British Library.

Microsoft Press books are available through booksellers and distributors worldwide. For further information about international editions, contact your local Microsoft Corporation office or contact Microsoft Press International directly at fax (425) 936-7329. Visit our Web site at mspress.microsoft.com. Send comments to *mspinput@microsoft.com*.

Active Directory, ActiveSync, ActiveX, BackOffice, Encarta, FrontPage, Microsoft, Mobile Explorer, MSDN, MSN, Outlook, PivotTable, PowerPoint, Visual Basic, Visual C++, Visual InterDev, Visual J++, Visual Studio, Win32, Windows, and Windows NT are either registered trademarks or trademarks of Microsoft Corporation in the United States and/or other countries. Other product and company names mentioned herein may be the trademarks of their respective owners.

Acquisitions Editor: Juliana Aldous
Project Editor: Anne Taussig

For all my friends, old and new

Contents at a Glance

Table of Contents

Part III   Technology

Acknowledgments

This book is unlike any I've written in the past. Rather than communicating my ideas and opinions, I'm communicating Microsoft's vision for knowledge management. That's what you're really interested in learning, after all. That leaves me with a whole lot of people at Microsoft to thank, as this book is more or less an executive summary of documents and information they produced.

Some of the information, particularly case studies that Microsoft made available to me, is unattributed. Even though the authors are unknown, I'd like to thank them anyway. To the authors of the following case studies, my sincerest gratitude for producing well-written study material and allowing me to use it in this book: Foster Parents Plan of Canada, British Petroleum, California Pizza Kitchen, Connect Austria ONE, HarperCollins Publishers, JD Edwards, KPMG, Microsoft Developer Network, Microsoft Direct Access, Microsoft Expense Tracking, Microsoft HeadTrax, Microsoft HR Web, Microsoft Performance Reviews, Microsoft US Sales, Nabisco, Siemens Business Services, Snapper Power Equipment, South Australian Government, Snyder Healthcare Sales, Toys R Us, University of Texas, and World Economic Forum. My gratitude also extends to the companies that participated in these case studies.

In addition to case studies, I've captured the best information from a handful of Microsoft white papers and presented it here in this book. The authors of those white papers deserve a special nod as they're the early innovators, the folks who are guiding Microsoft's vision for knowledge management. These include Matthias Leibmann, program manager with World Wide Technical Services, who authored *A Way to KM Solutions* along with Mukesh Agarwal, Howard Crow, Per Vonge Nielsen, and Michael Ohata. A similar Microsoft white paper, *Practicing Knowledge Management*, was equally useful in preparing this book, but this paper is unattributed. Thank you, whoever produced this thought-out guide to knowledge management. Last, a document called *Digital Dashboard Business Process Assessment Guide*, produced for Microsoft by InfoCal, is the basis for a lot of information in this book. My thanks to the folks at InfoCal (*http://www.infocal.com*) for producing this document.

This book's editors might be last in these acknowledgements, but they're certainly not least. Without the editors, this book would never have happened. They prodded me to finish. They ensured that the text made sense and that the thoughts were complete. They kept track of tiny little details that boggle the mind. In particular, I'd like to thank Anne Taussig, the book's project editor and one of the sharper individuals I've met, as well as the copy editor, Anne Owen, and the technical editor, Allen Wyatt. Also, Juliana Aldous, acquisitions editor, and Tracy Thomsic, content manager, were there from the very start, showed great patience, and were in the largest part responsible for this book existing in the first place. Thanks to both of you for everything.

Introduction

Snapper Power Equipment Company is a leading producer of yard-care equipment. For half a century, the Georgia-based company produced lawnmowers, tillers, garden tractors, and snow blowers. Snapper products are known for quality, and, for many decades, Snapper was the category leader. The company has been around long enough to witness a simple industry become crowded and utterly ruthless under the pressures of mass-market competition. It's in that environment that Snapper decided to overhaul its sales force. Instead of selling its products to 30 distributors, Snapper reorganized to sell to thousands of dealers—directly.

During the last decade of the twentieth century, the lawnmower market changed. The average American lawn was shrinking. Homeowners were spending less time maintaining their lawns. Moreover, Snapper's competitors were flooding the market with lower-quality, lower-priced lawnmowers, reducing the company's profitability as it tried to remain competitive. By the middle of 1997, Snapper had expanded its sales force from 10 to 65 people, who were servicing accounts from local hardware stores to megastores such as The Home Depot.

The results were disappointing. Snapper's paper-based ordering system, which worked fine with 10 salespeople and 30 distributors, collapsed under the weight of the larger organization. It couldn't keep up with 65 salespeople and thousands of dealers. Salespeople lugged around huge catalogs and price books containing information on more than 2,000 products. After taking orders, they hastened to the office to type and submit them. Errors were common, particularly in McDonough, where separate computer systems maintained the company's ordering, manufacturing, and processing data. Employees shared data by passing around disks or retyping information as required. Quality and customer service were suffering. According to Howard Jones, Snapper's MIS director, "We were struggling to react quickly to the marketplace, and we were losing money. We were not getting orders into the factory or product out of the factory in time; we were getting the wrong orders; we were dropping orders. Dealers didn't have what they needed from us, so they were selling something else. Lawnmowers are all about floor space. If it's not there on the floor, you can't sell it."

Snapper recognized the problem and, to remedy it, developed a sales-force automation system that leverages existing investments in technology and combines them with new technologies. Their new information network links the sales force, plant managers, marketing directors, and financial planners together, creating a single, continuous loop of real-time information that helps the company turn on a dime. From a single, familiar user interface, salespeople walk customers through an online ordering process, enter account information, file expense reports, and collaborate with customers and associates.

The transformation is remarkable, almost inspirational. Demand now drives the production processes. Manufacturing adjusts production on a daily basis to reflect the marketplace's changing demands, which the marketing department better understands because of real-time access to important data. Jones explains, "Without this technology giving information access to rank-and-file workers, decisions have to flow through a very hierarchical chain of command. The further away you get from customers, the fuzzier those decisions get. This solution lets us keep decisions close to the employees who are touching customers [in] the real world. We make decisions where the data is freshest, and the rest of the company can stay in step."

Snapper has unwittingly built the beginning of a knowledge-management system, a new approach to managing information that allows organizations to develop exciting tools that supplement the tried-and-true. The result is an integrated system that allows organizations to manage, optimize, and take advantage of the information coursing through it. This introduction describes knowledge management to you. I urge you to take action because, as Bill Gates explains in his book, *Business @ the Speed of Thought,* "In a Darwinian business world, the quality of an organization's [knowledge-management] system helps determine its ability to sense change and quickly respond, thus determining whether it dies, survives, or thrives." Will your company thrive in this environment?

KNOWLEDGE MANAGEMENT

Knowledge-management systems get the right information to the right people at the right time, provide them with the tools for analyzing that information, and give them the power to respond to the insight they glean from that information—all at lightning speed. As shown by Snapper, knowledge-management systems enable manufacturing to adjust production to meet demand, based on real-time information from the sales force. It enables just-in-time delivery of supplies and products, as retailers query the company's inventory and the company queries suppliers' inventories of raw materials. It also eliminates the countless hierarchies of red tape that impede day-to-day business. I'm speaking of paper-based systems that slow business processes; centralized decision-making that wastes the knowledge and experience of the workers who are closest to products and customers; and poorly connected computer systems that prohibit departments from sharing information.

Knowledge management is a discipline that treats *intellectual capital as a managed asset*. Knowledge management isn't a centralized database that contains all the information known by an organization's workers. It's the idea of gaining business insight from varieties of sources—including databases, Web sites, employees, and business partners—and cultivating that information wherever it resides. Business insight comes from capturing information and giving it greater meaning via its relationship to other information in the company. And to allay fears, knowledge management is not about making plug-and-play workers, dispensable because all they know is recorded for the next person who fills their shoes; it's about delivering information to *knowledge workers*, partnering culture, business processes, and technology to make businesses and people successful. Many factors contribute to the recent interest in knowledge management:

- Companies' valuations depend less on their fixed assets than on their management skills and how quickly they adapt to changing business climates. More than at any other time in history, investors value companies based on what they know.

- Trends toward leaner, meaner organizations result in employees who take what they know with them when they leave the company. Thomas H. Davenport and Laurence Prusak call this phenomenon *corporate amnesia* in their book, *Working Knowledge* (Harvard Business School Press, 1998).

- A global economy in which information travels at lightning-fast speeds is an important factor. In the last 50 years, economies have changed from labor-oriented, production-valued systems to intellectual and skill-valued systems. In *Intellectual Capital* (Doubleday, 1997), Thomas A. Stewart notes that in the United States, production workers accounted for only 34 percent of the workforce in 1980, as opposed to 57 percent in 1940 and 76 percent in 1900.

- Technology itself makes a strong contribution. The ability for technology to capture data, information, and knowledge has far outpaced knowledge workers' ability to absorb and analyze it. But it has also evolved to a point that allows companies to achieve Microsoft's vision of *knowledge workers without limits*. In this vision,

Microsoft's approach is to focus technology on the source of companies' knowledge: knowledge workers.

■ The existing ways of doing business are constantly under attack, more so now due to rapid changes in economies. Businesses must respond more quickly. The old ways of doing business and the old tools—such as TQM, Reengineering, and Activity Based Costing—don't cut it any more. Companies now understand that managing knowledge as well as the innovative processes is the way to remain competitive in a ruthless, fast-paced business climate.

Every company implements knowledge management differently. Each has unique knowledge assets and unique challenges within their organizations. Each has different processes and measures success in different ways. Therefore, knowledge-management solutions are unique to the companies that implement them. (Answers don't come in a box.) The following figure illustrates the key issues that companies deal with when they implement a knowledge-management solution. Not only must companies identify their knowledge assets, they must identify and overcome cultural barriers to knowledge management. They must align their knowledge-management solution with their business processes. Last, by applying the technology to the right problems, they enable knowledge workers. Each part of this book, "Organization," "Process," and "Technology," addresses these issues.

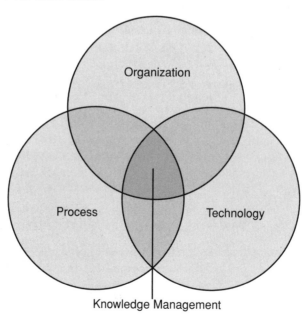

Knowledge management

Organization

Chapter 1, "Knowledge Sources," helps you accomplish one of the most difficult aspects of implementing knowledge management: identifying the company's knowledge assets. As you'll learn, there are three key places to look for knowledge. First, business data is hard facts: databases. At the next level is information, the result of analyzing and interpreting business data. It's the value that people add to data when they add their own experiences and ideas to it. Information is *explicit*. Examples of business information include e-mail, voice mail, and presentations. As you'll learn, at their own peril, many businesses rely solely on business data and information to make decisions rather than relying on knowledge, which comprises implicit experiences, ideas, insights, values, and judgments. Knowledge is dynamic and hides in places like business processes. The only way to harness knowledge is through collaboration, which is why Microsoft's knowledge-management initiatives focus on collaboration.

Identifying knowledge assets is only half the battle, however. With few exceptions, most companies indicate that cultural issues are their greatest barriers to implementing a knowledge-management solution. Employees tend to spend a lot of energy cultivating their knowledge to distinguish themselves in the organization. Of course, you've heard the phrase *knowledge is power,* and, in an organization that fosters this kind of spirit, companies encourage people to hoard what they know. In addition to people who hoard knowledge, another group of people is afraid of innovation and considers adopting technology a bit risky. Chapter 2, "Organizational Barriers," describes how to overcome these barriers through old-fashioned leadership and evangelism.

Process

Any knowledge-management solution must align with a business' processes. Thus, the effort begins by examining the company's processes for strengths and weaknesses, looking for ideas about where knowledge management will have its greatest impact—the biggest bang for the buck. Places to look include the four key business processes for which knowledge management has real, practical benefits:

- Product/service design and development. (See Chapter 3, "Product Design.")

- Customer and issue management (See Chapter 4, "Customer Management.")

- Employee management/development. (See Chapter 5, "Employee Management.")

- Business analysis and planning. (See Chapter 6, "Business Planning.")

Technology

At Microsoft TechEd 99, Bob Muglia announced that Microsoft was pursuing its vision of *knowledge workers without limits* with four key initiatives: digital dashboards, Microsoft Exchange Web Storage System, wireless connectivity, and intelligent interfaces. The last part of this book, "Technology," describes each of these initiatives:

- *Digital dashboards* give users one familiar place to go in which they can share knowledge and gain insight from important business information. Digital dashboards are built with Microsoft Office 2000 using open standards such as HTML and XML. They provide a rich environment for displaying and organizing information with which knowledge workers are already familiar.

- *Exchange Web Storage System* seamlessly integrates information from varieties of sources and allows knowledge workers to access that information from already familiar user interfaces. It combines the functionality of the file system, the Web, and a collaboration server, providing a single location for storing and managing information. Information in the Web Storage System is accessible via products you already use today, Microsoft Office 2000 and Web browsers, as well as from within your digital dashboard.

- *Wireless solutions* allow knowledge workers to access information anytime from anywhere. New types of mobile devices—such as phones, pagers, tablet PCs, and handheld computers—ensure that they can access the information they need when and where they need it.

- *Intelligent interfaces* enable knowledge workers to interact with computers in more natural ways. Types of intelligent interfaces include natural language processing, handwriting recognition, and speech recognition. Microsoft continues to make significant research investments in each of these innovations. Also, Microsoft recently announced ClearType, which is a display technology that brings the quality of LCD text up to par with printed text. ClearType promises to make technologies such as electronic books a reality.

The goal of these four initiatives is to pour a firm foundation for building knowledge-management solutions. The success of knowledge management depends on users' interaction with the company's information, so the initiatives enable them to use tools with which they are already familiar without requiring them to learn new ways of working. These initiatives also allow businesses to leverage existing investments in technology as well as existing sources of information, delivering information to users from every source that's relevant to them. Finally, these initiatives ensure that users who need information have access to it, whether they're using computers plugged in to walls or getting quality time on their favorite airline.

Initiatives are one thing, but the application of specific technologies is another. The appendix in this book, "Technology Roadmap," describes how Microsoft positions each of its products in typical knowledge-management architectures. How do Microsoft Exchange and Microsoft SQL Server fit into a knowledge-management scenario? What products do you need to evaluate and deploy in order to build a knowledge-management solution for business analysis? These are the types of questions that the appendix answers.

PARTNERING FOR SUCCESS

Knowledge-management principles and technologies are revolutionary. Are you convinced that you need to implement them in your company? Perhaps, but knowing and doing are different things. No two companies are alike because they use different steps to get there, and they apply the technology in different ways. Moreover, although Microsoft sells an innovative platform for knowledge management, you'll probably need to look elsewhere for help with assembling the building blocks. Few companies have all the resources required to implement knowledge management; most need outside help to meet their requirements.

Microsoft helps. You can build on existing investments in technology, implementing knowledge management incrementally. Add the bits that meet pressing business needs first; then, build on those with technologies that add value to your solution. Microsoft helps implement those priorities by providing a flexible technology platform for knowledge management, by supporting an open architecture that allows companies to integrate new technologies with existing ones, and by continuously improving Microsoft Windows so that companies can adapt to growth and change quickly and inexpensively.

Equally important, Microsoft helps by fostering a premier network of partners that provide specific line-of-business solutions. This network provides businesses of all sizes a choice of partners that understand their particular business needs. By making such a wide range of choices available, Microsoft ensures that companies such as yours get the best solutions for their particular requirements. For these purposes, partners fit into one of the following categories:

■ Systems Integrators (SIs) design custom systems, from networks to specialized computers, using products from various hardware vendors. KPMG is an example.

- Independent Software Vendors (ISVs) create applications for narrowly defined line-of-business needs and markets. Cipher Systems and ChangePoint are examples.

- Solution Providers (SPs) assemble software to create best-of-breed systems. Forte Systems and Software Spectrum are examples.

Snapper and ECMS

Snapper tried to implement a knowledge-management solution. They built a sales-force automation system, but, according to a company spokesperson, "It was a total disaster. The system ... was taking up an unbelievable amount of disk space, causing us to continuously upgrade everyone's computers. Also, the information in it was inconsistent and often wrong. Finally, the application was so complex that it was very expensive to maintain." Snapper recruited the help of Enterprise Communication and Messaging Solutions from Columbia, South Carolina. The result of their efforts was a sales-force automation system based on Microsoft Exchange that allows customer demand and field sales to drive production.

Partners such as Enterprise Communication and Messaging Solutions focus on particular aspects of knowledge management: workflow management, collaboration, or other technologies. They have more expertise, passion, and knowledge about their core competencies than companies trying to be all things to all people, and they certainly build better solutions than companies trying to do it all. Microsoft provides the platform, and partners combine the building blocks into complete knowledge-management solutions. You benefit with a lower total cost of ownership, increased interoperability, and an accelerated return on your investment.

Solution Providers

Microsoft Certified Solution Providers are companies that Microsoft certifies to offer services and solutions built using Microsoft products. The strict requirements for joining this program guarantee that you're working with highly qualified professionals. They provide a variety of products and services, including consulting, training, technical support, systems integration, product implementation, and custom application development. Locating an MCSP for your business is easy. Do one of the following:

- Visit *http://www.microsoft.com/referral*.

- Visit *http://www.microsoft.com/industry* to locate MCSPs that provide products and services for your particular industry.

■ Call (800) SOLPROV in the United States and Canada. Outside the United States and Canada, contact the nearest Microsoft subsidiary.

Not all MCSPs *get* knowledge management, but Microsoft does maintain a network of those that do. Open *http://www.microsoft.com/industry* in your Web browser. This Web page lists a variety of partners who understand knowledge management, and it describes the industries for which they provide goods and services. Additionally, it shows which technologies—of those described in Part III, "Technology"—and which Microsoft products each partner understands." Many partners can help with other aspects of your infrastructure, too, including electronic commerce and business operations.

Sources of Information

For more about Microsoft's knowledge-management initiatives, see *http://www.microsoft.com/business* and *http://www.microsoft.com/industry*. Several books give knowledge management more academic treatments, and I refer to them often:

■ *Corporate Memory: Strategies for Knowledge Management (Intellectual Capital Services)* (Dimension Publishing)

■ *Sense and Respond: Capturing Value in the Network Era* (Harvard Business School Press)

■ *Working Knowledge: How Organizations Manage What They Know* (Harvard Business School Press)

■ *Information Rules: A Strategic Guide to the Network Economy* (Harvard Business School Press)

Working Knowledge: How Organizations Manage What They Know is the ultimate academic guide to knowledge management. This book analyzes knowledge management as a business science. Thomas H. Davenport and Laurence Prusak are two highly respected authors with visionary insight into knowledge management in the business world. This is the one knowledge-management book I keep by my side.

Note that much of *Knowledge Management Strategies* is based on Microsoft white papers and case studies. Its purpose is to describe Microsoft's vision for knowledge management, after all. For the case studies you see in this book, you can often find more detail and more complete case studies on Microsoft's Web site or from your Microsoft account representative. For more information about the case studies in this book, I refer you to the two URLs near the beginning of this section.

MOVING FORWARD

This book is your wakeup call. I'm encouraging you to evaluate your company's knowledge-management system and, more specifically, your company's need for knowledge-management systems that empower your knowledge workers. British Petroleum, HarperCollins Publishers, Motorola, Nabisco, Siemens Business Services, and many other companies join Snapper in leading the way to smarter, more nimble businesses that no longer think *inside out*. These companies are more responsive to customers, employees, and suppliers. Best of all, these companies are all thriving. Before continuing, diagnose *your* company's ability to metabolize knowledge, by asking these questions:

- Do you learn, from anywhere in the company, about bad news quickly?

- Can you assemble virtual teams from separate departments and geographies?

- Can you capture and analyze customer feedback electronically?

- Can you quickly deliver customer feedback to employees who can fix problems?

- Can you capture and analyze customer-buying patterns?

- Can you determine which groups of customers are most profitable for you?

- Do you adjust production to meet demand on a daily basis? Weekly? Monthly?

- Can you collaborate with your customers and vendors?

In this book, I don't burden you with techno-babble that requires a computer dictionary to translate. This book is at the 10,000-foot level for senior IT decision makers and line-of-business people. Senior IT decision makers are responsible for identifying strategic applications for the business and aligning IT with fundamental business processes; they include chief information officers and vice presidents and their direct reports who are responsible for IT strategies. Line-of-business people are interested in how IT solutions maximize business efficiencies. I do make some assumptions about you, however. You understand basic networking concepts. You understand the role of the IT department and its infrastructure. You're familiar with current technology, its trends, and recent developments. I don't assume that you're familiar with deploying specific products and technologies, however.

My hope is that this book will help you better understand your company's needs and how you can apply Microsoft products to those needs. If I've done my job well, this book will leave you with many more questions than you had before reading it. I encourage you to send them to me at jerry@honeycutt.com. I'm fascinated by how companies use Microsoft technologies and will consider your stories for future editions of this book.

Part I

Organization

Chapter 1

Knowledge Sources

Knowledge hides in people's minds and in the company's processes;
finding and tapping into your company's knowledge sources
is your first big hurdle.

Knowledge management turns experience and information into results. According to sources at British Petroleum, knowledge is inexpensive and easy to replicate, but capturing it is not. In other words, identifying the knowledge sources to capture in a knowledge-management system is tricky; therefore, I address this issue right up front in this book.

This chapter suggests where you should begin. It describes a possible needs assessment. It identifies personal, team, corporate, and external knowledge sources, and it recommends specific situations that you must improve in order to build a successful knowledge-management system. For example, a fractured infrastructure, one in which clients don't interoperate well, should be a top priority for improvement. Another example of resources that require improvement is islands of information, where users in one part of the company can't exchange knowledge with users in another part of the company. Last, this chapter closes by making some recommendations for how to capture these knowledge sources in your knowledge-management system. This chapter assumes no technical wizardry, as it speaks to these issues on a 10,000-foot level.

DESIGN GOALS

A successful knowledge-management design has the following goals (see Figure 1-1 for an illustration):

- **Focus on the critical information**   With so much information coming from so many sources, knowledge workers often spend hours sorting through various materials in order to find one key point. A knowledge-management system helps solve information overload by delivering focused, vital business messages through the use of filters, user-specified categories, and summaries. Vital, high-level information can be accessed through relevant business reports.

- **Integrate information from a variety of sources**   A knowledge-management system integrates information from a variety of sources. Key business messages from corporate applications, Internet and intranet sites, team folders, and personal files can all be organized and viewed easily on a well-designed system.

- **Leverage the knowledge of others**   Knowledge-management systems enable knowledge workers to leverage what each other knows. As corporations become more global, collaboration increases in difficulty. Whether located in the office next door or on another continent, workers can use the system to locate and communicate with experts, collaborate on projects, or research corporate presentations and documents. Digital dashboards, which you learn about in Chapter 7, rely on Microsoft collaboration tools.

- **Work with the same information, in the office or on the move**   Knowledge management enables knowledge workers to make efficient and effective business decisions regardless of location. Nearly 44 million people traveled for business in 1998, up 14 percent from 1994, and the average business trip lasted about 2.5 days (*The Road Not Taken*, Bronwyn Fryer, Inc. Magazine Technology #2, 1999). All this travel means that knowledge workers are often away from their company's networks, their teams, their customers, and the Web. With digital dashboards built using Microsoft tools, information from any source, including favorite Web sites and shared public folders, can be viewed and used with or without an Internet connection.

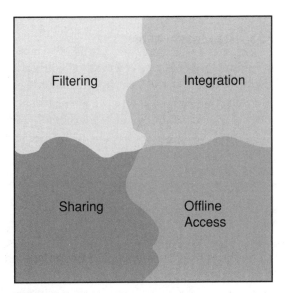

Figure 1-1. *Knowledge-management goals.*

NEEDS ASSESSMENTS

Needs assessment is a balancing act between managing end-user needs and maintaining the overall business strategy of the project. The needs-assessment part of the process is often conducted in tandem with researching the available information resources in order to assure a rapid development process, so I discuss it up front. Knowledge-management systems are an excellent way to bring together information and business applications from disparate sources in an integrated, customizable, and interactive environment. Needs assessment aims to clarify which information resources will yield the greatest impact as a part of the system.

Knowledge-management projects tend to start with a very limited focus and then grow. The focus of the project will determine its chances for success. Too often, as additional stakeholders (see Chapter 2, "Organizational Barriers," to learn about building a team of stakeholders) provide requirements and specifications, the project becomes increasingly complex, and cultural issues begin to pile up. This added complexity often makes it difficult or impossible to deliver an end-to-end system in a reasonable time. In addition, these projects often involve multiple iterations, so it is important to focus on those components that add the most value. The important thing is to not let the project get out of hand.

> ## KNOWLEDGE MANAGEMENT ADVISOR
>
> IT Advisor for Knowledge Management helps you evaluate your company's knowledge-management systems. It focuses on three key aspects of these systems: people and the value of their knowledge; processes, technologies, and their value; and business relationships, including customers and partners, and their value. This tool walks you through needs assessment and planning in order to help your company make the best use of its existing and future technology investments.
>
> At *http://www.microsoft.com/solutions/km*, Microsoft provides IT Advisor for Knowledge Management free of charge. Note that two versions of the advisor are available. The first is an online version. The second is the Desktop Edition of IT Advisor for Knowledge Management. The latter is the most useful, as you can refer to it over time and don't have to rely on access to Microsoft's Web site to use it.
>
> I recommend that you go no further in your processes before walking through the advisor. It's also useful to keep it around and to update its contents as your company progresses. Also, make sure you look at the help files for additional needs assessment and planning information. I tell you this only because the program is easy to use, and you'd probably not venture into the help system otherwise.

Business Goals

Because Microsoft's knowledge-management technologies are so flexible, the temptation to solve every problem and present every type of information in a knowledge-management system can lead to *feature creep* and a lack of focus. By clearly laying out which business objectives need to be supported by a knowledge-management system, you guide the needs assessment, prioritizing components. A system built on clearly defined business goals can, in the long term, reinforce business priorities to users. For example, if a particular business metric—such as customer satisfaction in a particular market segment or an organizational value such as training—is highlighted throughout a knowledge-management system, users will have these company initiatives in the forefront of their minds.

Business Processes

Although a demonstration of sample digital dashboards and open brainstorming helps generate ideas for content, considering the types of information used frequently helps prioritize those ideas. To identify these, walk through the various business processes of decision-making, and ask, "What pieces of information are needed to make different decisions?" Boiling it down to this level forces people to consider what information is absolutely necessary. The following characteristics are hallmarks of information that is useful in a knowledge-management system:

- Information that is used consistently

- Information with strategic relevance

- Alerts where timeliness is of the essence

- Paperless storage areas that are accessed frequently, such as a forms library

Usage Characteristics

Once the types of information are identified for inclusion in a knowledge-management system, focus on how the information is used. Usage characteristics are the final aspect of needs assessment. The results of the usage characteristics assessment will have the most profound effect on the technical architecture of the solution. In addition, a failure to meet this set of needs will certainly result in inconsistent usage of a knowledge-management system. Consider the following issues to determine how the various sources and types of information are used:

- Does the information need to be available offline? This will depend on the job classification of the individual end users. Make sure that the pilot group reflects the needs of the corporation as a whole in this need. Microsoft Outlook, Microsoft Exchange Server, Microsoft SQL Server, and Internet Explorer provide the ability to take virtually any information offline.

- Is the information read-only? While a knowledge-management system built using Microsoft products dynamically enables knowledge workers to find information easily, it is advisable to limit the ability to write to certain information sources. If all the underlying applications have been written to the Windows Distributed Networking Architecture (DNA) and support the security model of the Microsoft Windows NT and Windows 2000 operating systems, access rights will not be an issue. Environments with heterogeneous security methodologies can be difficult for users, requiring them to log into multiple applications.

■ Must the user be able to change data when offline? If data needs to be posted offline, a methodology needs to be derived for storing the entered data offline before it is synchronized to the server. Outlook, Exchange Server, and SQL Server support this type of data entry and can be synchronized with other databases to ensure data integrity between information stores.

■ How current does the data need to be? Very often, up-to-the-minute data is not as important as having availability offline. While Microsoft products support up-to-the-second information gathering and distribution, network bandwidth, financial-information security, and client storage capacities are tradeoffs that need to be considered.

■ How must the information be customized and to what degree? The type of information—such as personal or business information—might dictate the extent of customization. Personal information, such as e-mail and day-to-day project files, generally requires a high level of customization based on geography and personal preferences, while business information can generally be customized based on the user's organizational role. Also, the extent of customization depends on the users' ability to manipulate how information is seen and its arrangement. Finally, filtering of information based on target audiences and organization of information sources also play into this issue of usage.

User Needs

The greatest challenge might be in educating the sponsor, stakeholders, and pilot group on the opportunities offered by a knowledge-management solution. For example, most people are unaware of the rich data-analysis capabilities in the combination of Office 2000 and SQL Server 7. Therefore, it is important to demonstrate the variety of capabilities at the beginning of needs assessment. A good starting point for the needs assessment is the Digital Dashboard Starter Kit, which provides a set of sample digital dashboards for a variety of different roles and industries. For more information, see Chapter 7, "Digital Dashboard." Using examples specific to the company's industry engages participants and provokes further investigation into the solution.

Depending on the organization, the types of information and functionality of a knowledge-management system will vary. Some specific examples include:

■ Automated notification of events based on strategic goals

■ Relevant industry news

- Financial reporting with in-depth analysis

- Project tracking and reminders

- A specific line-of-business application such as sales-force automation

- Customer information—both external and internal

- Business analysis

- Personal calendar, electronic mail, and tasks

- Weather, traffic, and other external news feeds that might affect business

The following chapter, "Organizational Barriers," also recommends that you add lifestyle information to the knowledge-management system. This type of information can encourage people to use the system.

INFORMATION RESOURCES

In most cases, much of the information that is needed to produce a good first-generation knowledge-management project already exists within a company. Companies must be able to present information in an interactive and integrated manner. In some cases, existing information infrastructure can be enhanced to deliver significant business value at a minimal additional cost.

It is essential to work with stakeholders and information-resource owners to identify information assets that can be tapped. Most information sources can be found within the company. Often these resources reside somewhere on a mainframe or in a data warehouse. In other cases, the information may be in a semi-structured format or on the Web.

Collaborate with information-resource owners to get buy-in and assistance with operational, host integration, and support issues. Information-resource owners will often play a key role in planning ongoing support and administration of a knowledge-management infrastructure. Furthermore, information-resource owners are often helpful in determining and discovering where the best data/information sources are located and in what format.

A knowledge-management system is not just one system or one application. It is an integrated view of multiple applications. It is an intuitive, flexible tool that uses Internet standards to deliver data access, collaboration, and analysis applications to knowledge workers. When evaluating what types of information to include on a digital dashboard, make sure to look at broad categories of applications to get a mix of all the items that a knowledge worker uses during the day.

Personal

Knowledge workers tend to keep a large amount of information on their hard drives for reasons of privacy and security. The most common items are e-mail and calendar items. These items never appear on traditional server portals, and this differentiates a digital-dashboard solution built using Microsoft products from a run-of-the-mill portal. By taking advantage of Outlook Today (see Chapter 7, "Digital Dashboard"), it is quite easy to include personal information.

Team

To foster innovation, teams are working increasingly across organizational and geographic boundaries. Exchange Server helps capture what these teams learn and facilitates collaboration among dispersed teams. Knowledge-management systems built on Outlook 2000 provide knowledge workers access to the tools they need to share documents, discussions, tasks, and other productivity tools.

Team information resources can vary from ad hoc sharing of documents and discussions to more structured, process-based applications. All of these applications can be included in a knowledge-management system. In addition to capturing shared information, a knowledge-management system can take advantage of tools such as NetMeeting, with which people can collaborate face-to-face over an intranet or the Internet, and Windows Media Services, which is particularly useful for broadly distributing training material and sharing best practices.

Corporate

Corporate information systems store much of the most crucial information that can be included in a knowledge-management system. These information systems are distinguished from other resources because they are usually controlled by the IT group and have a highly organized system of maintenance and security. The presence of legacy data and the massive requirements placed on these systems makes corporate information resources the most difficult to deal with. The payoff for working through this information is a greater understanding of the business, its markets, and its customers.

Unfortunately, knowledge workers are often inundated with paper-based weekly, monthly, and quarterly reports from these systems, which are often mainframe- or ERP-based systems. These paper-based reports are expensive in many respects. They do not allow customization. Readers cannot easily locate data. Worst of all, there is not a way to intelligently filter information based on business rules to alert people of problems or opportunities. If you move these systems into tools such as Office 2000 and Office Web Components, they can provide more interactive reporting and the value of these resources can be realized.

Various lines of business require different performance metrics. Traditional sales and marketing organizations need to *slice and dice* sales and profitability figures by each product, part, region, and individual. Conversely, a manufacturing firm will focus its performance measurements on yield, throughput, cycle time, and inventory levels. Today's Internet firms have introduced new measurements such as unique visitors, reach, average minutes per month, and pages viewed per day.

External

Knowledge workers must stay abreast of world events, publications, legislative affairs, and competitors. Resources of information can be a dynamic repository of hyperlinks, a news and stock ticker scrolling across the screen, a targeted news wire that covers a specific industry, or a bulletin board or issue forum. With knowledge-management systems based on Office 2000 and Web standards, integration of external content such as news feeds is a very easy task. Due to the broad availability and variety of external information, a customization engine such as that on MSN is often advisable.

RESOURCE IMPROVEMENT

Many significant issues will arise when working with corporate information resources, as these are the most complex resources and often housed in legacy systems. Great strides have been made to improve the tools available for solving some of these issues. Minor upgrades to information systems can often yield significant increases in the usability of information. The following sections address these issues:

- Information islands
- Poor reporting
- Fractured infrastructures
- No common taxonomy

These sections also mention a number of technologies that you learn about later in this book. For more information, see Chapter 8, "Microsoft Exchange Web Storage System."

Information Islands

One of the most common problems is that information is stored in multiple systems across a corporation (see Figure 1-2 on the next page). Depending on the type of information, various tools are available for consolidating information across a wide variety of systems. For example:

- **Accounting, customer, and other line-of-business data**   This type of data is often stored in a variety of systems. In large corporations, accounting data from different divisions might even be in different systems. SQL Server includes a feature called Data Transformation Services (DTS), which consolidates data from a variety of modern and legacy databases, thereby enabling better reporting and easier understanding of the business as a whole. This service can also reduce the expensive and time-consuming process of manually *rolling-up* financial reporting. The DTS Package Designer provides a graphical environment for working with data in a variety of systems.

- **Documents, discussions, and Web pages**   This type of information is generally more dispersed than corporate data as it is generated in a more ad hoc fashion. Microsoft Site Server includes a sophisticated mechanism that can search across documents, discussions, internal and external Web sites, and SQL Server databases. With this capability, knowledge workers can confidently search across the entire corporate memory. Once this type of cross-company catalog is established, it is easy to integrate into a digital dashboard.

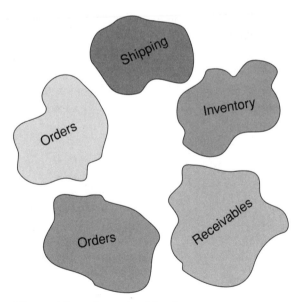

Figure 1-2. *Information islands.*

Poor Reporting

As discussed earlier, paper-based reporting is inadequate for moving through large amounts of data to spot trends. The combination of Office 2000 and SQL Server allows knowledge workers to connect directly to business data and conduct any number of sophisticated analyses. The Microsoft Online Analytical Processing (MSOLAP) technology enables this sophisticated and flexible analysis. With the MSOLAP features included in SQL Server and Microsoft Excel, knowledge workers can use familiar tools to conduct sophisticated analyses of corporate data.

Fractured Infrastructure

When knowledge workers need to communicate with subject matter experts or their teammates, a fractured collaboration and messaging system should not get in the way. E-mail, discussion, and shared document folders are the most efficient way of communicating in today's mobile and global environment. Exchange Server provides a scalable platform that can grow to support any sized organization's messaging and collaboration needs in a consistent seamless fashion. In addition, teams can use tools such as the Microsoft Team Folders Wizard to build and deploy team-based applications that are built on the same central Exchange-based e-mail infrastructure. This guarantees that knowledge workers get the resources they need to get their jobs done efficiently.

No Common Taxonomy

The most significant roadblock to the effective integration of information resources for knowledge-management systems is the lack of a common way of labeling or tagging information. Often, one business unit may call a metric by a name that differs substantially from that used by another part of the organization. A similar problem occurs when two departments refer to two metrics by the same name. This is usually a cultural problem. The best way to get this resolved is to work to a common taxonomy. However, in some cases this kind of information can be stored in a person's profile and display the information in their taxonomy of choice.

DEVELOPMENT

Development methodology is best left to your IT department, and this chapter doesn't address this topic in detail. It does discuss some issues that are critical to a successful implementation of a knowledge-management system, though, so that you're asking the right questions when you talk to the IT department. First and foremost is documentation. Documentation is a fundamental component of any development project, especially how data and information are linked together. These data flow processes and their underlying data models must be thoroughly documented, including the timing of the information as it moves from location to location.

There are three key roles in implementing knowledge-management systems. Depending on the amount of work that is needed on the information resources, responsibilities can be shared across the roles. The first role is focused on finding, normalizing, and preparing information resources for inclusion in a system. Another role is focused on developing or refining the four to five applications that are components of the system. Finally, the third role attends to the user interface representation, user interface extensibility, and offline synchronization.

Development will take place in a series of steps. As prototypes and betas are shown to users and stakeholders, additional requirements are defined, taxonomies are refined, and a general consensus on business priorities is reached. Early in the process, more attention is paid to the presentation of the information; in later revisions, there is a slightly higher emphasis on data issues in order to compensate for the greater emphasis on user interface issues in the first stages. The last stage prior to deployment is testing. Testing of a knowledge-management system is a little different from that for most classes of applications and, because this is also a cultural issue and closely related to the project's stakeholders, I address this topic in the following chapter, "Organizational Barriers."

GETTING THE RIGHT HELP

Going forward with knowledge management, your company will build expertise. Having the expertise in your IT department in advance is not likely, so you'll need help planning and implementing your plans. Learn from other companies' experiences. Many companies comment in case studies that they had a number of false starts, as many as three major efforts failing, before bringing in outside help. In most of these cases, the primary reason for the initial failures was that the company just didn't have the knowledge base required to implement a successful knowledge-management system. Whether you're evaluating Microsoft products or not, you need a good knowledge base.

Microsoft makes finding help easy through its Microsoft Certified Solution Provider (MCSP) program. To qualify for this program, third-party

continued

Getting the Right Help *continued*

companies must employ Microsoft Certified Professionals (MCPs) who have demonstrated a level of technical expertise that allows them to develop and deliver solutions based on Microsoft products. Microsoft judges an MCP's competence by using certification exams that the company develops. These consultants receive the same training that Microsoft provides its own engineers, so they are well acquainted with Microsoft products and how to best deploy them in a variety of scenarios. They also have full access to Microsoft's development and product support groups; therefore, they can respond quickly. MCPs run the gamut from Microsoft Certified Systems Engineers (MCSEs), who are essential network and operating system gurus, to Microsoft Certified Trainers (MCTs), who are certified to teach others about Microsoft products.

Microsoft's Business site, *http://www.microsoft.com/business*, has an MCSP locator that helps you locate the best MCSP for your needs. The locator asks you a variety of questions, including the size of your infrastructure and the type of solution you're planning, and then recommends MCSPs in your area. It's up to you to interview and choose the right MCSP, however, as they're independent companies that are beyond Microsoft's influence. This site also includes information about how to interview and choose an MCSP—valuable information, particularly for smaller businesses that usually have only one shot at getting things right.

WRAP UP

Knowledge management is about leveraging the corporate memory and, in order to accomplish that goal, the project must identify and improve the company's various knowledge sources. Here are this chapter's highlights regarding knowledge sources:

- Needs assessments help you identify the goals for your knowledge-management project as well as the various knowledge sources it must capture.

- Information sources include personal, team, corporate, and external. Knowledge-management systems built on Microsoft products provide flexible solutions for capturing knowledge from all of these information sources.

■ Your company must improve some resources including those in information islands or that are limited due to a fractured infrastructure. Poor reporting and a lack of a common taxonomy are also problems that a knowledge-management system must improve.

Taking Stock

1. Where is the information and knowledge in your organization?

2. What are you trying to accomplish with a knowledge-management system?

3. What processes are you trying to improve with a knowledge-management system?

4. Do users have specific needs that a knowledge-management system must address?

5. Do knowledge-workers have particular usage patterns such as offline usage for which the knowledge-management system must account?

6. Is your corporate data and information well defined? Do all of the company's IT departments use the same taxonomy for that data and information?

7. Are your departments well connected so that they can share information?

8. Are users artificially separated by a fractured infrastructure?

ACTION PLAN

❑ Informally or otherwise, identify the goals you're trying to achieve.

❑ With the help of your IT department, conduct a needs assessment.

❑ Identify the personal, team, corporate, and external sources of information that must be in the company's knowledge-management system.

❑ Identify and plan to improve information islands, poor reporting systems, fractured infrastructures, and weak taxonomies.

❑ Cooperate with your IT department to create a development plan.

Chapter 2

Organizational Barriers

*To facilitate the success of knowledge management in your
company, break down cultural barriers in its way:
hoarding, resistance, and so on.*

Knowledge-management systems depend on companies' cultures and how well those cultures support the efforts of the people who produce the information in them. High-value content that an empowered staff produces is more useful in a knowledge-management system than the drivel that employees produce due to cultures that don't support sharing ideas openly—obviously. In addition, the more expensive human resources a company has or the more dependence a company has on sharing and reusing information, the greater benefit the company receives from fostering cooperation, instead of rewarding knowledge hoarding or resistance to change. That's the first key for breaking down organizational barriers to knowledge management: *reward positive behavior, not negative behavior.*

To that end, knowledge management is largely about people. Culture and behavior is important. You must encourage employees to take the time to learn before jumping on new tasks, for example. You've heard it before: Reward failure so that you encourage employees to take risks. So, as you read this chapter, keep in mind that technology enables knowledge-management systems, but knowledge management is just as much about leadership (yours), culture, and behavior. You must create a culture that is conducive to sharing information, finding it, and creating knowledge. This chapter points you in the right direction. It helps you overcome some of the most common cultural barriers, particularly those witnessed in Microsoft case studies. You can find a fuller treatment of this subject in *Working Knowledge* by Thomas H. Davenport and Laurence Prusak (Harvard Business School Press, 1998). Leading business books also help you overcome cultural barriers to technology in general.

Figure 2-1 shows an overview of the processes you can use to avoid certain classes of cultural problems. The idea is to get users involved early and, as the system evolves, create a feedback loop that captures corporate and user requirements.

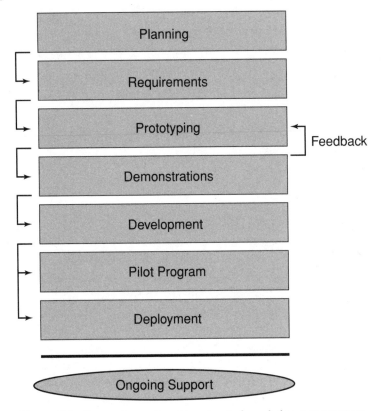

Figure 2-1. *Preventing cultural barriers to knowledge management.*

FOCUSING ON USERS

An overriding principle is collaboration with the people who will use your company's knowledge-management system. Throughout the case studies you read about in this book, an essential ingredient to success is communication with users. For example, British Petroleum, one of the largest petrochemical companies in the world, gave users information about why the company was deploying its knowledge-management system. It used newsletters and road shows. It published deployment plans and technical standards. It educated its users. After the company implemented its system, it gave users even more information over an intranet and a half- or one-day training course that taught them how to use their new system. Before dropping knowledge management in users' laps, the company answered the big five journalistic questions—who, what, how, why, and where—eliminating surprises.

Communication with users will yield all sorts of feedback. You'll hear about the importance of usability. Employees won't use the word *usability*, however. They might express uneasiness about learning a new system or they might balk at the change. When they do anything like this, they're pleading for you not to create a system that sets them up for failure, whatever failure means to them. The following sections address some of the feedback you might hear and ways you can focus on users as you plan a knowledge-management system. For example, most users are primarily concerned with filtering information so that they get what they need, without all the noise. Other users might be more drawn to your knowledge-management solution if you include personalized information in it, such as weather and traffic reports. The success of public Internet portals, such as MSN and Yahoo, illustrates how important personalization is to users.

BRITISH PETROLEUM SNAPSHOT

British Petroleum recruited the Microsoft Certified Solution Provider Digitalpeople to help the company become more responsive, to increase employee productivity, to create a "true learning organization," and to lower the cost of ownership. British Petroleum's knowledge-management solution included 33,000 desktop computers "including IBM and Dell computers", 500 workstations, and 1500 servers "including Compaq and Dell servers". On these systems, British Petroleum deployed a range of Microsoft

continued

British Petroleum Snapshot *continued*

operating systems, productivity applications, server products, Internet applications, and development tools, including the following:

Operating Systems	■ Microsoft Windows 95
	■ Microsoft NT Workstation 4.0
	■ Microsoft NT Server 4.0
Productivity Applications	■ Microsoft Schedule+ 7.5
	■ Microsoft Office 95 7.0b
	■ Microsoft Office Professional 95 7.0b
	■ Microsoft Project 4.1a
Internet Tools	■ Microsoft Internet Explorer 3.02
Development Tools	■ Microsoft FrontPage 95 and later
	■ Microsoft Visual Studio
Server Products	■ Microsoft Exchange 5.0
	■ Microsoft Proxy Server 1.2
	■ Microsoft SNA Server 1.0
	■ Microsoft SQL Server 6.5
	■ Microsoft Systems Management Server 1.2

Making It Easy to Use

Usability is probably one of the greatest barriers to a successful knowledge-management system. A difficult-to-use system sets knowledge workers up to fail. According to Mark Post, director of global knowledge management technology development at KPMG, a knowledge-management solution must allow people to easily access the knowledge and information they need, when they need it—or they simply won't use the system. KPMG had to shift its corporate mindset from one of knowledge hoarding to one of knowledge sharing to ensure its success. "Knowledge management needs to be integrated into everything that everyone does; it needs to become part of the way we work," says Michael Turillo, KPMG's international chief knowledge officer.

To facilitate that cultural change, KPMG created an easy-to-use, Web-based knowledge portal called KWorld. This unified interface provides buttons that allow KPMG employees to navigate quickly to news stories and KPMG's internal content; to the Microsoft Outlook messaging and e-mail client for e-mail, scheduling, and task management; and to Microsoft NetMeeting conferencing software for real-time document sharing or videoconferencing. "In the KWorld environment of messaging, knowledge sharing, and collaboration, we're able to get the right people collaborating and working together in a very powerful way," says Turillo. Because the company created a system that is so easy to use, the chances of its success are good: KPMG employees are likely to use the system and actually begin to depend on it.

Usability is a discussion that's far beyond the scope of this book and one that's best left to your IT department. Microsoft is one of the best examples of a company that builds successful, usable products, though; you can learn a lot of concepts just by using the company's products. Also, numerous books on the subject are available at your local bookstore, including a few from Microsoft Press. A final note: If you involve actual users in the process from the get-go, you're likely to build a usable knowledge-management system. Feedback is the best indicator for usability.

Handling the Big Changes

Usability is one thing, but what about those users from whom which you're pulling out the rug? Big changes for those users include your taking away software, changing their mail clients, or even changing their platforms. A more extreme example is taking over management of non-managed desktops, a process that requires adjustment for everyone involved. In these cases, users are going to express initial concern, but communication and participation will get most of them past these hurdles. Be patient. Some users will never make it over these hurdles, however. As harsh as it sounds, this might be a good time to replace employees who don't adapt well, particularly in fast-paced business climates.

KPMG is an example where big changes went over well. Responses to the new system were varied, particularly in parts of the company that were heavy Macintosh users. They were concerned about moving to PCs. The company proved these concerns unjustified, however, as the customer-satisfaction surveys exceeded 98 percent and internal measures of service availability exceeded 99 percent. "They don't miss their old Macintosh machines any more," says Ashton. "Broadly speaking, the users understood the value of standardization and common ways of working. In particular, they knew that it would lead to better service and support, so that there was generally very good buy-in to the changes. We enjoyed executive support at the most senior levels, which is critical in a project like this."

A key to KPMG's success was communicating the reasons for and the value of these changes to users. Once they understood how important interoperability was to the success of the knowledge-management system, everyone got onboard. Telling is one thing, but showing was another. After users witnessed for themselves how the system would improve their lives—users saw dramatic improvements in the e-mail system's reliability, for example—they never looked back.

Addressing Personal Needs

The previous chapter, "Knowledge Sources," described how to perform a needs assessment so that your knowledge-management system captures the right information sources. To some degree, that has less to do with identifying the information required to run your business and more to do with drawing users into your portal. Although it does seem tangential, lifestyle information encourages employees to use your knowledge-management system on a regular basis. Information such as weather, sports scores, and traffic reports make your knowledge-management portal attractive to its users. Such data makes the site interesting and more practical for everyday life. Examples of lifestyle information include the following:

- Weather reports
- Traffic reports
- Stock tickers
- Travel bulletins
- Industry news
- Announcements

As with all things, balance is tough to measure and tougher to achieve. Too much lifestyle information can chew up network bandwidth or distract employees from their responsibilities. How far you're willing to go with this depends on your distinct situation. Some choices are common sense—don't encourage Internet-based radio by including links to radio sites in your portal— but evaluating how much network bandwidth that part of your portal uses will require the help of your IT department. In general, personalized information should draw in users but not interfere with their jobs.

PERSONAL PORTALS

Microsoft recently announced a personal knowledge-management portal for Outlook 2000. This portal works with MSNBC to provide updated news, weather, and business information in Outlook Today, Outlook 2000's opening screen. In addition to this personalized content, Outlook Today displays the user's schedule and task list. Still other companies are jumping on the bandwagon by building innovative personal knowledge-management portals with features such as advanced searching capabilities, categorization of e-mail, and much more. For more information about personal portals, visit *http://www.microsoft.com/office.*

Eliminating the Noise

When the word gets out that your company is implementing a knowledge-management system and users learn that it will be based on Web technologies, you're going to get a predictable reaction from some of them. They're used to the Internet and the fact that 90 percent of everything they see is noise. Filtering that noise in order to find useful nuggets of information is difficult for anybody, no matter how well they know the Internet. However, in a controlled system that's built for specific business goals, eliminating the noise is easier, and you should communicate this fact.

J.D. Edwards didn't want to talk, analyze, or think about knowledge management to death; it wanted to build a system that would deliver immediate results. And it certainly didn't want to build an elaborate knowledge repository that nobody used. The company wanted to build a well-integrated system that delivered the information that knowledge workers needed to do their jobs while filtering out the rest. For J.D. Edwards, the first step was to identify the people and processes that most directly generated revenue: the sales team. Knowledge-management specialists spent months interviewing the sales force, finding out what they need to know to do a better job every day. What did they read? What did they bring to client meetings? How did they get product news? How did they keep up with the competition? This was the stuff of a good knowledge-management system.

The company's knowledge managers developed an enterprise-wide set of core competencies for organizing the company's knowledge. The key to success was organizing around topics, issues, and the information that people need to do their jobs. But organizing knowledge this way was a challenge because it required cutting across departmental boundaries. J.D. Edwards met this challenge by forming *knowledge centers*, logical groupings of information that are independent of department origin. A dedicated knowledge-management staff oversees the presentation of information within each center. This staff reads, selects, tags, and directs information into the J.D. Edwards Information Network. The company believes that this staff eliminates millions of documents that would help no one in the company. Because employees are able to find the information they need and no more, they can produce more positive results.

J.D. EDWARDS SNAPSHOT

J.D. Edwards used Microsoft Consulting Services and META Group to build its knowledge-management solution. Their system puts all of the company's critical information in a single location from which knowledge workers can get the right information when they need it. The company is working smarter, working faster, and providing better information to its employees and clients. J.D. Edwards' knowledge-management system was built using the following products:

Operating Systems
- Microsoft Windows 95
- Microsoft Windows NT Workstation
- Microsoft Windows NT Server 4

Productivity Applications
- Microsoft Office 97
- Microsoft Office 2000
- Microsoft Internet Explorer 4
- Microsoft Outlook 97

Development Tools
- Microsoft FrontPage
- Microsoft Visual Studio

Server Products
- Microsoft Exchange Server 5
- Microsoft Site Server 3
- Microsoft SQL Server 7
- Microsoft Systems Management Server

CHOOSING A PILOT GROUP

From the beginning, getting the right people involved in designing the project is important. Those choices set the tone for the entire project. And choosing the right group of people to pilot the project is one of the most important decisions you will make. The best group of users is usually determined by the culture of the company or organization. Keep in mind that word travels fast and these users' initial experiences will get around to employees who will be using the system later. Therefore, make it count.

Speed, momentum, and strategic relevance are three key issues to investigate when considering the construction of a pilot group. Because knowledge-management systems are related to so many other systems, both business and technological, it is important to maintain focus when developing the pilot and learning from the experience. Choosing a group with strategic stature in the organization can ensure that the project's success will be both visible and measurable. The sales department is a good example. Some general pointers for identifying potential pilot groups include the following (illustrated in Figure 2-2):

- Select a visible group, as the pilot group can generate a greater cultural shift with greater visibility. Although a knowledge-management system is not exclusively an executive tool, the influence of executives makes them good pilot candidates. However, because executives also have different needs from those of knowledge workers, it is important to investigate the needs of a more diverse group through a tandem pilot.

- Choose a group that is representative of the strategic direction of the company. Knowledge-management systems will often have a broad effect on the way information gets delivered to the organization. Working with the information and user communities that have the greatest potential value will guarantee the best long-term impact.

- Look for groups where valuable knowledge is being lost. For instance, a sales group that does not properly capture information on customer visits and winning sales strategies can serve as a pilot with a very measurable impact on revenue.

- Consider the types of information the group uses. If the information is stale, erroneous, or held in antiquated systems, it can slow down a pilot significantly.

- Use multiple pilot sites in larger, more global organizations. Bandwidth, cultural, and information issues in larger organizations differ greatly from country to country, and not understanding these issues may hurt the long-term effectiveness of the project.

- Beware of groups with high barriers to sharing information. It is important to determine, through background interviews, the levels of software experience and skill, readiness for technology acceptance, and any reluctance that may exist among key stakeholders. In many cases, the *owners* of information or knowledge are hesitant to share. Once the benefits of the pilot are realized, people will become more amenable to sharing information.

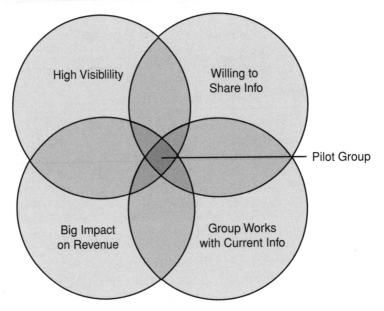

Figure 2-2. *Choosing pilot groups.*

Sponsors

Enlisting a high-level sponsor—usually the CEO, president, or business-unit leader—is imperative. Look toward the top of the company's organizational chart for a suitable sponsor, one who can lead—perhaps you. A sponsor can help gather the necessary resources for the project. A knowledge-management system should also be built for these sponsors, primarily for cultural reasons. Sponsors who endorse and use knowledge-management systems foster a collaborative, team-based approach to sharing information and knowledge. They can remove many perceived risks of using the system. They set an example.

Stakeholders

In addition to the pilot group of users and the sponsor, a working team of stakeholders can provide motivation for implementing a knowledge-management system throughout all levels of the project. A good number of stakeholders is between 5 and 10 people. They include subject matter experts, usage characteristic experts, data/information producers, and IT professionals. Too many stakeholders can make it hard to balance the many needs of a large constituency, though. The stakeholder team includes the following roles:

- **Business Owner** Defines the strategic goals of the pilot and ensures focus on the end goal of enhancing business productivity.

- **Technology Infrastructure Owner** Gives perspective on the technical development and maintenance of the systems and the long-term impact of digital-dashboard solutions in the organization.

- **Pilot Group Representative** Brings the knowledge workers' perspective to the stakeholder team. This person should focus most on the difficulties of adapting end users to the system rather than on the final benefits.

- **Information-Resource Owners** Represents the people who manage information resources that will be available on a digital dashboard. Typical resources are customer-relationship information, accounting data, and training and development content.

Smaller businesses often have more organic natures and less complex infrastructures. In these situations, broad stakeholder teams are not necessary and pilot projects can be managed in a more ad hoc fashion. Additionally, some individuals can fill more than one of these roles in such organizations. Many companies have built successful knowledge-management systems as grass-roots efforts, rather than well-organized projects with complex lifecycles.

PROTOTYPING THE SYSTEM

An early prototype of the knowledge-management system is extremely useful, especially for getting people onboard early in the process. The development cost is somewhat minimal, and a prototype helps to expose holes and inconsistencies in the information. Those holes can be filled before the working system is constructed. Presenting the prototype and findings to the stakeholder team in a group setting allows each member of the team to see, for the first time, other members' preferences for business metrics and application targets. By meeting as a group, stakeholders are less likely to accuse each other of not understanding the key measurements of the business. In addition, a group setting helps solidify the team agenda rather than allowing individuals to break off from the group focus.

DEMONSTRATING TO END USERS

This step of the process is intended to prepare the end user community for a new knowledge-management system. Part of this step is to help end users prepare for the necessary cultural transformation, and part is to prepare them for the technology implementation. This step is the first opportunity for stakeholders to compare their vision of the system to the needs of the end users. It allows users to better prepare for the changes that are coming down the road, helping them feel more involved in the process. If end users agree with the stakeholder vision, system adoption becomes much easier. This process should have three components:

- An outline of the high-level goals of the program and long-term vision.

- A statement from the sponsor underlining the importance of sharing knowledge to the company and a reiteration of how the system will improve this function.

- A demonstration of the knowledge-management system.

Organizations should not create the expectation that the first iteration of a knowledge-management system is going to solve everyone's problems. Instead, they should focus on how it can assist knowledge workers in solving certain classes of problems with information delivery and collaboration. The demonstration typically shows four to five example applications that will soon be put into production. The goal is to stimulate end user thought about system application and how it might be extended to assist in solving similar problems.

Ongoing Collaboration

Flashing around this new knowledge-management system is worthless unless the stakeholders are open to feedback and criticism. In fact, consider formalizing the process of showing the prototype and collecting feedback from users. That sends a powerful message to knowledge workers: "We're building a knowledge-management system to help you be more successful and we want you to help build it." Some companies collect feedback about their knowledge-management system using a simple public folder. A team composed of information-resource owners, support people, the sponsor, and the development team can monitor discussions. This serves not only as a support mechanism but also as a learning device for capturing the best and worst facets of a digital dashboard for later versions.

Reviews by Stakeholders

Throughout this process, it is important to assimilate the feedback from various groups, to meet with stakeholders to review the knowledge-management system, to explore reactions to the initial demonstration to end users, and to refine software presentation and content. These design reviews should be attended by the entire stakeholder group in order to maintain agreement regarding the major system-design goals and business metrics.

Testing a digital-dashboard solution (see Chapter 7, "Digital Dashboard") is a little different from testing most other classes of applications. The most likely source of error (and the most troublesome to detect and correct) is in the quality and timeliness of data/information compiled by the system. Therefore, it is critical to include subject-matter experts as testers. This is because testers who are not subject-matter experts usually cannot determine the difference between good information and bad information.

It is also important to have a trainer and at least one support person perform some of the testing in order to begin familiarizing themselves with the system. Additional *train the trainer* or *train the support desk* instruction might also be necessary. Depending on the complexity of the system, end user documentation or some other instructional materials might improve the success of your solution.

WRAP UP

Some companies have more significant barriers to overcome before they can successfully deploy a knowledge-management system. Key ways you can overcome these problems include the following:

- Get users involved in the process early so that they buy in to it and they have a chance to express their needs for the knowledge-management system.

- Make the knowledge-management system easy to use to help ensure that knowledge workers do indeed use the system.

- On an ongoing basis, communicate with users so that you don't surprise them. Make sure they understand the purpose and the importance of the system.

- Address users' personal needs by adding lifestyle information to the knowledge-management system, which draws users into it and makes it more attractive.

- Carefully choose a pilot group to test the system, realizing that this initial group of users' impressions will affect how well the remaining users accept it.

- Find a sponsor for the knowledge-management system who's in a position to set an example for the rest of the company's knowledge workers.

- Create a team of stakeholders that can guide the knowledge-management project. Stakeholders include the sponsor, the business owner, the technology-infrastructure owner, the pilot-group representative, and information-resource owners.

- Early in the process, demonstrate the new knowledge-management system to users and collect their feedback so the company can improve the system.

Taking Stock

1. Does your company's culture reward knowledge hoarding?

2. Are your company's employees resistant to technology changes?

3. Can you leverage your company's existing culture to entice employees to embrace your new knowledge-management system?

4. Have you identified a pilot group that will put your knowledge-management system on solid footing during its early days?

5. Does your project have a sponsor? What about stakeholders?

6. Does your company regularly involve employees in major decisions, such as deploying a knowledge-management system, or will this be a cultural change?

ACTION PLAN

❑ Identify knowledge workers and processes that directly affect revenue.

❑ Talk with those users, getting them involved early in the process.

❑ Prepare a newsletter or even regular events during which you discuss the company's knowledge-management initiatives.

❑ Single out a sponsor whose support will provide financing and set an example for the rest of the company.

❑ Identify key employees as stakeholders, and schedule regular meetings with the stakeholder team so that they work as a group.

❑ Develop a prototype for the system that helps you communicate a vision.

❑ Demonstrate the prototype and early versions of the knowledge-management system to users and prepare to accept positive and negative feedback.

Part II

Process

Chapter 3

Product Design

Take better products and services to market with integrated groups of professionals; knowledge management empowers product design.

A key to successfully designing products and services is collaboration across the multiple groups of disciplines involved in the effort. Collaboration helps make sure that the product or service meets the customer's needs by capturing input from all of the groups that have a stake in doing so or have valuable insight into that process. For example, sales, marketing, engineering, design, and other groups can all share best practices in design and development. Knowledge-management systems provide the methodology as well as the best way to capture those best practices.

Some types of businesses are better suited to collaboration around product and service design. These businesses are typically, but not always, technology businesses. Consulting, research-and-development oriented, and engineering businesses are prime examples. Historically, technology businesses have been early innovators and have paved the way for others. Examples of businesses that aren't technically oriented but still benefit from collaboration include the food service and consumer goods industries. The case studies in this chapter are from both segments, and the subjects are KPMG International, a technology company, and Nabisco, a consumer goods company.

Collaboration brings ideas and information together to help projects move forward more quickly and efficiently. People become more aware of what other people in the organization know and don't know. Ideas get around, reducing the duplication of effort and increasing cooperation between departments. Some departments in some organizations might not be so willing to share what they know, however. Chapter 2 discusses the techniques for working on that problem. Once you get knowledge management working in your projects, the measure of its effectiveness includes product success rates, changes in cycle times, and the amount of rework that must be done once a project is finished. Keep these points in mind as you read the rest of this chapter.

SERVICE DEVELOPMENT

KPMG is evolving itself into a unified, global company with a mission to "turn knowledge into value" for its international customers. Executives at KPMG realized that they needed a highly scalable knowledge-management solution that would help the company reach that goal and allow 100,000 employees in 160 countries to collaborate—even with offices that are oceans apart. "Our business is all about information," says KPMG CEO Paul Reilly. "If we can't demonstrate that we can manage the experience of our own people, then we're not showing clients a very good example of why they should hire us."

KPMG asked Microsoft Consulting Services (MCS) and Cisco Systems to help the company create and deploy KWorld, a Web-based knowledge-management system that combines technology with business practices. Executives at KPMG predict that KWorld will help position the firm as a world leader in providing international tax, consulting, financial advisory, and assurance services. "KWorld is the largest global investment our firm has ever made," says Reilly. "We're betting our future that this is going to leap us ahead of our competition." KWorld is a primary example of how a service company can use collaboration to offer more to customers.

KPMG SNAPSHOT

KPMG built a knowledge-management solution that would differentiate itself from its competitors. They wanted to lead by example. The solution, KWorld, allows knowledge workers to leverage information from all of the company's employees. The goal is to make better, well-informed decisions and to unify the KPMG offices throughout the world. With the help of Cisco

---

continued

KPMG Snapshot *continued*

Systems and Microsoft Consulting Services, KPMG's solution was built with the following products:

Operating Systems	■	Microsoft Windows NT Server
Productivity Applications	■	Microsoft Office
	■	Microsoft Internet Explorer
	■	Microsoft Outlook
Server Products	■	Microsoft Exchange Server
	■	Microsoft Site Server
	■	Microsoft SQL Server
Hardware Products	■	Cisco 7500 Router Series
	■	Cisco Catalyst Ethernet Switches

Setting an Example

KWorld has an easy-to-use, Web-based knowledge portal, which you learned about in Chapter 2, "Organizational Barriers." From the KWorld interface, people can tap into the accumulated corporate knowledge of KPMG to get the content they need in the context of the project on which they're working. For example, as illustrated in Figure 3-1 on the next page, a KPMG consultant assigned to a new project can log on to KWorld and search for all consultants with expertise in a specific industry, technology, country—or all three. The consultant can find relevant information to assist with proposals, engagements, statistics, and reports, and the worker can read threaded discussions about related topics. KWorld allows KPMG consultants to learn from the collective experience of hundreds of thousands of skilled colleagues through a single, integrated knowledge-management solution.

Providing Better Service

Working closely with MCS and Cisco, KPMG developed and deployed KWorld to 47,000 employees in just nine months. Although KWorld has been in place only since June 1999, KPMG executives have already noticed significant changes in how clients view the firm's services and how employees work with those customers. Before the KWorld rollout, for example, KPMG found itself at a disadvantage against a competitor that said it could provide better service than KPMG because of its collaborative solution. Those tables have turned quickly

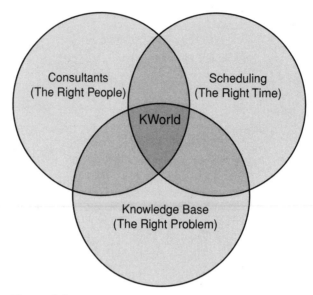

Figure 3-1. *KWorld.*

and dramatically, thanks to KWorld. KWorld is now able to offer KPMG clients a collaborative environment where client knowledge and KPMG knowledge can come together to benefit both.

Employees embrace KWorld because it gives them the information they need when they need it. In fact, according to Reilly, KPMG partners and employees around the world are clamoring to be connected to KWorld, which had been deployed in four countries as of the fall of 1999. As the company continues to deploy KWorld, executives expect to see a remarkable change in the quality of KPMG goods and services. "Because of knowledge management, we're going to market with better products than we would otherwise have, with better service, and with a more integrated group of professionals; people are able to inform one another and engender an environment where their services are being refined more quickly and responsively with regard to clients' needs," says Bernard Avishai, director of intellectual capital at KPMG.

By continuing to improve KWorld's environment, KPMG will be better positioned to capture, protect, and use its employees' knowledge to provide customers with the best global services possible. KPMG executives expect dramatic results from the KWorld system. According to Reilly, "KWorld is all about increasing our revenues by having access to solutions and knowledge, increasing our margins through access to methodologies, and increasing our market share by being a leader."

Standardizing Design

To build KWorld, KPMG chose Microsoft and Cisco Systems components, which met the company's demand for tight integration. The Microsoft Windows NT Server operating system forms the foundation of KWorld and is designed to work seamlessly with the Microsoft BackOffice family of server products, which KPMG also uses. Microsoft Site Server hosts the company's intranet, Microsoft SQL Server provides relational database management, and Microsoft Exchange Server delivers messaging and collaboration capabilities. On the hardware side, KPMG employs the Cisco Systems 7500 router series and Catalyst Ethernet Switches, which integrate with Microsoft products to provide reliability and scalability.

In the process of standardizing on Microsoft and Cisco products, KPMG replaced 13 messaging systems and integrated at least seven knowledge-management systems that were precursors to KWorld. This standardization allows employees to communicate electronically without worrying about whether their messages arrive safely, as mail travels through a single system. In addition, a unified messaging system helps KPMG deliver the right information to the right person at exactly the right time, which often means the difference between success and failure. The system also simplifies the jobs of IT administrators by giving them fewer systems to support and maintain, thus lowering costs.

KPMG plans to deploy KWorld in 30 more countries by 2000, and the company is already planning for the next generation of KWorld. According to Bob Zeibig, the partner in charge of KPMG's Global Knowledge Exchange, the updated version of KWorld will include enhancements in security, navigation, and personalization. KPMG also plans to upgrade to the Microsoft Windows 2000 operating system to take advantage of Active Directory, giving administrators greater and more centralized control over content security and network performance. Cisco Systems will play a major role in that upgrade process, helping to ensure that the KWorld system can scale up to meet the needs of more than 100,000 KPMG employees. The strong compatibility between Cisco products and Windows 2000 will allow KPMG to take full advantage of the newer Microsoft operating system, providing dynamic network resource allocation to users who are running bandwidth-intensive applications. "KPMG chose Cisco not only for its proven track record, but because its products integrate with the Microsoft platform to give us scalable bandwidth, prioritization of network traffic, and resources," says Zeibig. "The Cisco products will be critical to the success of KWorld in the future."

PRODUCT DEVELOPMENT

When you think of product development, do you think of software, automobiles, or electronics? What about snack foods? Consumer goods companies use similar processes and methodologies to develop the latest chocolate craze as Microsoft uses them to develop the next great application. In a competitive and volatile snack food industry, developing products and getting them to market quickly are essential to success. For industry leader Nabisco, continually developing and producing products that people want to try is essential to the company's success, particularly because many snack foods are impulse purchases. Determining which product ideas to pursue and which to discard can significantly affect Nabisco's bottom line. One bad decision can result in millions of dollars of unprofitable research and development, manufacturing, and marketing. Nabisco must walk the tightrope between keeping product ideas flowing and sidestepping expensive failures.

To consistently create profitable products and keep money-losers off the shelves, Nabisco created Journey, a new product-development process that coordinates all project communications and establishes firm go/no-go hurdles for every project. Journey was built in a few months from off-the-shelf Microsoft software products. By enabling better communication and tighter project management, Journey is saving Nabisco millions of dollars annually by eliminating unsuccessful development efforts and expensive product-specific equipment.

From a knowledge worker's point of view, Journey consists of a series of Outlook forms, which are organized into categories such as project status, reports, activities, and supporting documents. When team members click a tab, they see the postings to that category for a specific project, generally as Office 97 files. For example, a project team member might write meeting minutes in Microsoft Word and send them to Journey, which posts the minutes for everyone to see and notifies team members that meeting minutes are now available. Another might submit project financials as a Microsoft Excel spreadsheet. A third might post a Microsoft PowerPoint presentation. Journey shows all team members a summary of this information; if people want more information, they simply double-click to access the complete file. Figure 3-2 shows how this very typical organization looks logically.

Because Nabisco is a premier marketing company, it promotes collaboration by putting powerful analysis tools on the desktops of its marketing staff and other knowledge workers. "The more tools and technology our knowledge workers have, the better we communicate, the smarter our decisions, and the faster we can get new products out the door," Klein says.

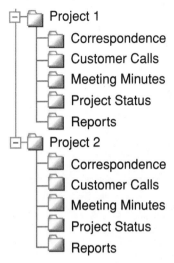

Figure 3-2. *Using Outlook forms to organize project information.*

Success Rates

Historically, Nabisco's new products followed a consistent pattern (see Figure 3-3 on the following page):

- One third were blockbuster successes.

- One third were mediocre performers.

- One third were under-performers, meaning they lost money.

The failures that got through the planning process usually did so because project champions managed to wiggle past guidelines that, if strictly followed, would have eliminated potential losers before they ever got to market. Nabisco management wanted a product-development process that left no *wiggle room* and provided a means for cross-functional teams to maintain constant communication.

Journey was built on Nabisco's existing infrastructure, namely Exchange Server and SQL Server on the back end; the Microsoft Office 97 suite, including the Outlook messaging and collaboration client, on the desktop; and the Microsoft Visual Basic 5 and Microsoft Visual C++ development systems. Because Office and Outlook were already in use, the need for extensive training and education was alleviated. Building Journey on top of this technology infrastructure saved months, maybe years, of development time and millions of dollars.

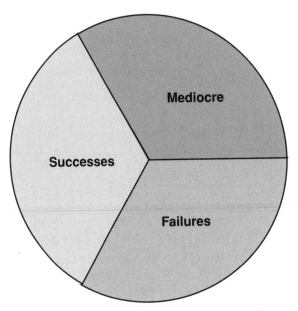

Figure 3-3. *Historical product success rates at Nabisco.*

NABISCO SNAPSHOT

Nabisco created Journey to better plan its products, giving them a greater chance of success straight from the start. The goal was to keep products that don't meet the company's stringent criteria from slipping through the cracks and to foster collaboration and knowledge sharing during the development process. Journey uses a combination of the following products:

Operating Systems
- Microsoft Windows
- Microsoft Windows NT Workstation
- Microsoft Windows NT Server

Productivity Applications
- Microsoft Office 97
- Microsoft Outlook

Development Products
- Microsoft Visual Basic
- Microsoft Visual C++

Server Products
- Microsoft BackOffice
- Microsoft Exchange Server
- Microsoft SQL Server
- Microsoft Systems Management Server

Project Repositories

One of the key benefits of Journey is that it acts as a central repository for all project data, from financial estimates to recent product scores to project timelines. As projects move along, Journey lets users know which milestones have been passed and which are coming up. This is typical project-management information.

Journey prescribes that every new product must have market research and financial tests performed at certain stages. At each stage, minimum scores must be achieved. This information is communicated through Exchange public folders, so everyone on the team knows whether a product made the grade or not. Then Journey prescribes the next step(s) and notifies the responsible parties. Before Journey, these issues could be skipped or fudged, but the Journey system establishes firm quantitative hurdles and go/no-go criteria of which everyone is aware.

Journey hides the complexities of the project (and the application itself) from users so they see only the information they've requested at that moment. However, on the back end, Journey is intelligently calculating scores, dispatching e-mail, updating schedules and budgets, posting reminder notes, and keeping track of thousands of details for hundreds of people. The application is written in Visual Basic and Visual C++, and it builds on standard capabilities in Exchange and Outlook.

Project Reporting

Team members and management can easily produce reports that roll up project data to create a macro-level view of all the company's development activities. "Journey gives us a full portfolio view of new development projects, any time someone wants to see it," explains Eileen Murphy, Nabisco's senior director for new product development. "Management can very quickly and easily see what we have in the pipeline five years out. Do we have enough new products coming out in the near term? In the long term? Do we have a gap between projects that will directly impact revenues two years from now?" Putting together or updating a rolling 18-month aggregate plan used to be an enormous task that involved checking with all project teams, tracking down numbers, and knitting information together manually. Journey does this automatically.

Collaboration

If problems arise during product development, Journey helps the team solve them quickly, by simultaneously engaging the resources of the whole team, as opposed to the old method of sequential problem solving. For example, during the development of a particular cookie product, the manufacturing team reported a problem: The product developed an undesirable texture during baking tests. The manufacturing team entered this problem into Journey as a discussion item, and Journey immediately notified the entire project team. Research and development got involved and offered a solution: add an ingredient to modify the texture. Another team member reminded everyone that the addition of an ingredient would require approval by the U.S. Food and Drug Administration (FDA) and a packaging revision. The packaging department got involved and made the change. The legal department obtained the FDA approval. In the end, the problem was solved in a short period of time (a few days) versus the old process that might have taken weeks or months to play out. This is in sharp contrast to handing the problem from department to department, none of which has all the information required to solve it; and eventually, everyone ends up in a series of long meetings that wastes valuable time.

This scenario isn't so different from what happens in a software company such as Microsoft. A test engineer reports a problem, such as a dialog box that displays data incorrectly, and then other departments collaborate to fix the problem as quickly as possible. The marketing department chimes in to make sure the development engineers understand the impact of the problem on customers so they can prioritize it properly. Product support flags the problem if the department sees it as a serious support problem. Other departments provide their insight. The company resolves the problem quickly because of the give-and-take that collaboration makes possible, which is not much different than the give-and-take that Nabisco's knowledge-management system makes possible when its employees troubleshoot their latest cookie product (see Figure 3-4).

Journey is helping Nabisco increase its success rate for product introductions to 100 percent. The company has managed to eliminate the one-third-failure bucket, and the staff is working to improve the one third of new products deemed mediocre performers. "You can really see the change in our new product mix since Journey," Murphy says. "We're making product decisions based more on knowledge and good business than on emotional attachment to favorite ideas. If things aren't going well for a new product, we know it sooner rather than later and can fix or cancel it."

Managed Costs

Journey makes extensive use of the public folders feature available with Exchange Server. Individuals can route e-mail messages—along with reports, spreadsheets, presentations, and other documents—to a public folder that is accessible by any number of authorized individuals. Everyone on that folder's list receives an e-mail message telling them something new has arrived. The public folder feature is useful for keeping many people abreast of project activities, facilitating collaborative communication, and providing a coherent trail of communication over long periods of time. A SQL Server database (currently about 250 megabytes) and a dedicated Exchange server take care of all the messaging. David Klein, director of marketing technology for Nabisco, says, "Exchange is a robust environment for developing collaborative applications like Journey. It has most of the capabilities you need for these kinds of applications, which saved us a lot of development time."

Figure 3-4. *Problem solving with knowledge management.*

Nabisco has made a whole-hearted commitment to 32-bit computing and has launched a corporate-wide migration to the Windows NT operating system, the BackOffice family of products, and Office 97 desktop products. Down the road, Windows 2000 and Office 2000 will be available to help the company simplify and centralize its operations.

Nabisco sees huge benefits in standardizing on a single technology infrastructure throughout the organization. "It takes a while to get there, but when you have a common infrastructure throughout your organization, you can roll out new applications much faster, minimize training, and increase users' productivity," explains Joseph Farrelly, Nabisco's executive vice-president and chief information officer. He says Microsoft applications are optimized to work together and are fully compatible, reducing costs. In addition, "The ability to quickly get new applications in users' hands delivers a very real business value," Farrelly says.

By standardizing on both hardware and software and purchasing in volume, Nabisco is lowering its total cost of PC ownership. All new applications take the Office 97 suite into consideration, utilizing power and capabilities already developed by Microsoft. Moreover, because the Windows operating system provides the same interface for all desktop applications, users can be more productive sooner and training costs are lower. "The Office 97 products are great products—truly superior to anything else on the market," Klein says. "We use features like the Microsoft System Management Server installer to speed up deployment, which translates directly into lower costs." He adds that the rich online help also benefits the bottom line. "The Office Assistant help system lets our users help themselves more," reducing helpdesk calls, Klein says.

Support from Microsoft has been crucial to Nabisco's deployment of both desktop and server-level products. "We are big users of Premier Support," Farrelly says. "We're really breaking new ground with some of the things we're doing, and Premier proactively assists us in our implementation planning stages, while ensuring that any issues are escalated as needed through the appropriate support channels."

Nabisco's standardized client-server infrastructure is allowing the company to rapidly create applications like Journey that help product designers respond more quickly to fast-changing customer tastes. After just seven months of use, Journey reduced trial budgets by a third, which means Nabisco is concentrating on a smaller number of products that the company believes will be sure things. Nabisco is also saving millions of dollars by avoiding projects that require huge investments in specialized equipment and training that can't be used across other products. Because Journey adds rigor to market research and other critical decisions, Nabisco is better meeting customer desires, boosting brand loyalty, and increasing sales. From now on, Nabisco can almost guarantee it will make money on new products by ensuring they're baking what consumers want.

WRAP UP

Product and service design is one of the most obvious uses for knowledge management. In this usage, development, marketing, sales, legal, and other departments collaborate to bring better services and products to the market. Ideas that the case studies in this chapter illustrate include the following:

- Knowledge-management systems that help companies deliver products and services are usually found in technology companies, the early innovators. But those kinds of systems are just as appropriate in other types of companies, such as those that deliver consumer packaged goods.

- Not only can service companies use knowledge-management systems to develop better services, but they can also use knowledge-management systems to coordinate, manage, and improve those services once they go to market.

- Standardizing on a single messaging and collaboration architecture helps ensure that users will be successful and makes the system more manageable in the long run.

- Collaboration allows product development companies to bring insight from its various departments together to produce results quicker than before possible.

- Implementing a successful knowledge-management system is often no more difficult than assembling the right set of off-the-shelf products.

- Well-designed knowledge-management systems can reduce product failures significantly and, as the case with Nabisco, can sometimes reduce them to zero.

Taking Stock

1. Does your company produce technology products or services?

2. Does your company provide a product or service that requires different departments to collaborate in order to deliver them?

3. If your company sells a service, do your current systems allow you to match the right people to the right jobs, accounting for schedules and skill sets?

4. Does your company have an automated system for forecasting the success or failure of products and services before sending them to market?

5. Do you know your product success rates, and are you happy with them?

ACTION PLAN

❏   Evaluate your current systems for product and service collaboration.

❏   Set realistic goals that you'd like to achieve, such as specific success rates.

❏   Working with each department that participates in the product or service's design, draft requirements for a knowledge-management system.

❏   When building your knowledge-management system, leverage existing products that will help you deliver a system that's better, cheaper, and faster.

Chapter 4

Customer Management

*Knowledge-management systems empower companies to
build more effective sales forces and to keep their
customers coming back again and again.*

No business succeeds without satisfied customers, and the only way for businesses to satisfy their customers is to build relationships with them. That requires companies to track customer relationships: their issues, buying patterns, and expectations. Good knowledge-management systems facilitate this process; for example, they help companies build a more effective sales force and help companies better support their customers after the sale.

The primary technologies that facilitate customer management are document tracking and collaboration. In this chapter, you learn about a variety of solutions from a variety of businesses that use these technologies.

Microsoft uses the principles you learn about in this chapter to keep better track of the depth and breadth of its customers. The company also supports its customers—*empowers* them is perhaps a better term—using online support. This chapter describes these systems as well as a few other systems that help businesses build stronger relationships with their customers. As you read this chapter, keep in mind how these companies measure the success of their knowledge-management systems. Are the customers satisfied? Are customers' needs captured in the company's products and services?

SALES MANAGEMENT

Keeping track of companies, customer contacts, and ongoing sales opportunities in a company as big as Microsoft can be a logistical nightmare. To help manage sales, Microsoft segments its U.S. sales organization into three main groups (see Figure 4-1):

- **Depth Accounts**—Organizations with 5000 or more computers

- **Breadth Accounts**—Organizations with 1000 to 5000 computers

- **Medium-Sized Accounts**—Organizations with 50 to 999 computers

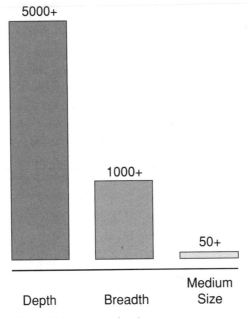

Figure 4-1. *Microsoft sales groups.*

A combined telesales and field-sales force handle all three of these customer types. "The field and phone reps are tied at the hip to serve their customers," says Patrick Gifford, director of corporate account sales (CAS). "They have to figure out how to leverage their own time and our partners' time to get the most revenue from their accounts." The telesales representative is responsible for surveying a large territory and knowing all the key decision makers in each account: the hardware and software they're using, the key Microsoft people involved, the key partners involved, and upcoming opportunities. They're calling these accounts all the time, sending intelligence to their selling partners, and proactively marrying partners into specific opportunities. The field sales representatives work specific issues that are more difficult to deal with over the phone, such as highly competitive situations, final contract negotiations, and service issues.

Lost Opportunities

Greg Enell, a Microsoft corporate account sales representative, got the word on a Tuesday afternoon that a key customer was shopping for a new messaging system but was already talking to a competitor. The company was a huge Microsoft Exchange sales opportunity, but Microsoft would have to work fast. Enell called his field representative, Ramsay Gamble, and put her on alert. He reviewed ATLAS, Microsoft's corporate opportunity database, to catch up on the customer's hardware and software inventory. He examined numerous spreadsheets that contained account, revenue, and partner information, and he discovered that his district's records on the customer were rough and outdated. They both recalled that the customer had a problem a year before and that technical support got involved; neither could remember the outcome. Additionally, their best customer contact was promoted in a recent reorganization. Things were falling apart for this sales opportunity.

When Microsoft's two-part sales organization was set up, the company thought that the ATLAS database would be the primary tool gluing the telesales and field sales forces together. But ATLAS has neither contact-management features nor offline-replication capability, which impairs field-sales representatives' ability to keep their records up to date. As a result, the two sales organizations had to cobble together a complicated web of private databases, spreadsheets, and e-mail folders. Each of the 18 field sales offices had its own way of organizing customer records, and individual telesales and field-sales reps maintained private records of customer visits, revenue opportunities, and partner engagements. To do their jobs, the sales force had to scurry to three or four different places to find data, synthesize it, and make decisions. Hours could be lost tracking down the right person or piece of information and then combining and reconciling three Microsoft Excel spreadsheets that didn't match up. Additionally, frequent requests from marketing and management for customer lists—by job title, geography, products used, and so on—for special mailings chewed up a lot of time.

Bringing It Together

Situations like this—working with no timely information—stressed out Enell and Gamble. Thus, working with a technology specialist, they created a solution: a customer-management system using Microsoft Exchange Server and Microsoft Outlook. "Outlook is on everyone's desk; we knew we needed something to help communication, and we couldn't wait for a long application development process," says Dale Goff, sales manager in the U.S. CAS organization. "We still have a lot of work to do to make it perfect, but I'm amazed every day at all the cool things Outlook can do for us." This knowledge-management solution has helped the company better manage its customers, and similar systems can help your business do the same thing.

Each district created an Outlook Contact public folder. Both the field and phone-sales representatives enter their customer contacts into Outlook or import their data from Excel spreadsheets and Microsoft Access databases. This becomes the common repository they use as a shared working database. Every time one of them (or anyone else in the company, for that matter) has contact with a customer, they enter the encounter into the Outlook public folder. Everything about that customer—e-mail messages, partner information, and problem information—is in one central place. No longer do sales representatives have to look in different places for intelligence about a customer, and the intelligence that's in the customer's public folder is likely more accurate as a result.

Everyone in the company has access to this information over the corporate intranet; thus, management can pull its own reports on customer activities. If the field manager for Southern California is asked by his boss, "How many customers are we currently negotiating with on an enterprise agreement?" he can go to the system and select the standard "Licensing View" of customer data without contacting each and every sales rep in his district. Also, when the marketing staff wants to invite all CIOs in a particular region to a special event, it can pull its own mailing list by selecting a "Job Title" view of the data, again without imposing on the sales force.

Day to day, the Outlook-based contact management system makes both the telesales and field sales forces far more productive. "I'm not constantly cycling my brain worrying about what I'm forgetting, going through mail and my calendar looking for loose ends," Enell explains. "I don't need to do that anymore. I just look in one place. I can view my outstanding sales opportunities by status, by products used, by partner, by competitor, by account expiration, or anything else. To pull any of this out of spreadsheets would take hours." Enell and his field partner Gamble customized an opportunity-tracking module within Outlook to help them keep track of sales opportunities by revenue, by partner, and so on. "When we sit down for our weekly phone meeting, we can now see in one place what the status of each opportunity is," Enell says. "Before, the information was scattered all over. On a weekly basis, we can cover three times the number of accounts during a two-hour call. I would say this tool is saving us four to six hours a week."

Field sales representatives can update information when they're offline, too. At least once a day, field sales representatives synchronize their laptop computers to the public folder using the record-level offline-synchronization feature of Exchange. This keeps the field folks up to date with all account developments that might have taken place elsewhere in the company. Because Outlook allows representatives to customize this offline synchronization, they can synchronize and sort only the accounts they're interested in—maybe 500 out of 4000 records. This makes the process faster and more effective for that representative.

Eating Dog Food

After about a year of use, the Outlook public-folder sales solution has dramatically improved communication between the field and telesales representatives. "Everyone's on the same page all the time," says corporate account representative Gary Zyznar. "If you don't know what's going on in an account, you haven't looked in the public folder." Zyznar used to keep his own e-mail folders to track account histories. If someone else was going into the account, he had to take the time to educate him or her first. Now, the data is there for everyone to see. He says the system has also relieved him of the onerous chore of backing up data. "We've eliminated many representatives maintaining many separate data centers of information. Today, it's all backed up in the central data center, saving us tremendous amounts of time and eliminating the chance that any one individual will lose or corrupt a critical customer record."

Zyznar's telesales partner, Parker Norwood, says he feels the system is saving the reps hours every week in information fire drills brought on by management's frequent requests for mailing lists. "Now management can pull these quickly without disrupting our work. We no longer have to generate month-end reports, nor see e-mail with these requests." Norwood roughly speculates that Outlook is saving 96 reps at least an hour a day. Plus, the lists are more accurate and up to date, so success rates for direct-mail pieces and invitations are much higher than in the past.

The Outlook solution has helped Microsoft work more closely with partners. Representatives can cut a particular view of an account and paste it into an e-mail message to a partner. It increases the frequency and accuracy of Microsoft's contact with partners, making them a closer part of the virtual team.

It's almost impossible to quantify how much money the system is saving Microsoft or how much additional revenue it's bringing in. "But having all the data in one place helps us make decisions faster," says Mike Simpson, corporate account representative. "Our turnaround time is dramatically faster, and management can access this data as fast as we can. Speed is important in sales, because we often need to move quickly—within hours—to take advantage of an opportunity. When a competitor makes a play, we need to be able to deliver a fast, accurate response. We can scan our database and quickly find other customers we might use as references. The great thing this system demonstrates to customers is that 'we're eating our own dog food,' as we like to say—that we're using our own tools to run our company and doing a great job of it."

GRASSROOTS SOLUTIONS

Microsoft's Outlook public-folder solution was a grassroots movement. Telesales representatives created contact-management systems in Outlook and shared them with their counterparts in the field. Goff thought this was a great idea but saw a need for consistency in the way these contact-management systems stored customer information. As a result, CAS set several standards for using Outlook and Exchange. For example, every district would maintain only one public folder, field representatives would synchronize with the public folder on a daily basis, and there would be several standard views of the data, although representatives were allowed to create custom views based on the standard ones.

To further ensure the success of the project, CAS provided a full day of Outlook training for all the representatives, particularly training for its contact-management features, and also appointed a "champion" in each district. The champion was the person who took the lead in promoting the proper usage of Outlook in that district.

Even though the system is still being polished, it became a functional, productive tool practically from day one. "We could have taken longer to think through the process and do more architectural planning up front, but we just jumped in and did the best we could," Goff says. "Speed was important; we didn't have time for a traditional development process. We opted to dive in and create a rough but usable product right away. There's no way could we have done this with other collaboration products. The average user can't touch some groupware products to customize them, but they can be up and running on Outlook in minutes—and manipulating views to their heart's content. That kind of hands-on, grassroots, take-charge empowerment is what Outlook is all about—and our experience is a great example of it."

INFORMATION LOOPS

Collecting contact information is only half the battle; completing the information loop by capturing customer feedback is the other half, the Snapper case study, which you learned about in this book's introduction, illustrates this part well. Snapper's first attempt at getting customer feedback on products back into the research and development cycle didn't go smoothly. The company looked to its sales force to provide a direct pipeline from customers into Snapper and to see where it could operate leaner and meaner. Snapper decided to eliminate the middlemen, the distributors that served as liaisons between Snapper and its thousands of dealers around the country. The intention was to bring Snapper closer to its customers and, of course, eliminate the cut that the dealers used to take. As a result, in 1997, the company upped its sales force from 10 to 65 people and threw them at thousands of dealers, ranging from mom-and-pop stores to superstores such as The Home Depot.

The problem was that Snapper's salespeople drowned in paperwork. Their paper-based sales and order systems worked fine for 30 customers but not 4500 customers. Sales representatives lugged heavy catalogs and price books around into dozens of dealer showrooms; they raced to record orders on paper forms and fax them back to Snapper, where they were keyed into an IBM AS/400-based manufacturing system. With such a workload, collaboration among salespeople suffered, too. There was no way a relatively small sales force could share ideas and customer knowledge using only telephones and fax machines. Snapper struggled to react to the marketplace and was losing money as a result. The company failed to get orders to the factory and didn't get products out of the factory in time. For that matter, the company got orders wrong and sometimes dropped orders. To make the situation worse, knowledge about the company's customers was on separate systems, and the only way to collaborate was usually to pass diskettes around or reenter data. Sales people didn't share best practices, and the company wasn't pleased with its customer service.

After a few misfires, Snapper recruited a Microsoft Certified Solution Provider called Enterprise Communication and Messaging Solutions (ECMS) to help build a knowledge-management system based on Exchange Server. According to Robert Ginsburg of ECMS, "Exchange is an extremely powerful messaging system with a very powerful directory system. It's also very scalable; you simply add servers and move folders around. And, very important to any company today, it's highly cost effective."

Like many knowledge-management initiatives, the move brought some dramatic changes to the way Snapper's sales force operated. Snapper believes this new knowledge-management solution will give its sales force an accurate, consistent, easy-to-use tool for taking orders, tracking orders through the factory, and moving product to dealers precisely when they need them. The company's knowledge-management system creates a continuous loop of information between the field and the plant, as illustrated in Figure 4-2. This ensures that information is accurate as well as timely. According to Snapper, "We get sales data quickly and react quickly—basically instantaneously."

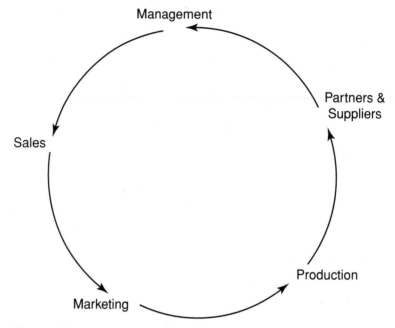

Figure 4-2. *Information loops.*

The company's knowledge-management system gives its sales representatives a single, graphical, point-and-click interface for walking customers through a graphical online product catalog, entering orders, reviewing extensive account information, scheduling their time, filing expense reports, sending e-mail to customers and colleagues, creating reports—managing all of the knowledge about customer interactions the sales force might need as well as carrying out other corporate tasks. Management can use the system to check up on sales representatives' progress and schedules to see, for example, how many cold calls they're making and how often they're calling on customers. Marketing can tap into the system to gather more knowledge about its customer base, to see what's selling, and to track how promotions are doing. Also, manufacturing adapts its production on a daily basis to what's happening in the field, driving their business processes off the same, shared customer knowledge base.

SNAPPER SNAPSHOT

With the help of Enterprise Communication and Messaging Solutions (ECMS), Snapper built a knowledge-management system that created a continuous loop between the company and its customers. Better communication between each of the company's departments, its customers, and its suppliers means that the company gets the right products on the shelves at the right time. Snapper's solution was built on the following combination of Microsoft products:

Operating Systems	■ Microsoft Windows NT Server 4
Productivity Applications	■ Microsoft Office 97
Server Products	■ Microsoft BackOffice
	■ Microsoft Exchange Server
	■ Microsoft SQL Server

REPLACING THE PAPER

A division of Snyder Communications Inc, Snyder Healthcare Sales is an outsource sales and marketing agency for healthcare companies. It provides trained sales representatives who make thousands of on-site calls to doctors' offices, clinics, and hospitals on behalf of drug manufacturers, delivering presentations that change prescribing behavior and drive product sales. It's a job that demands gathering timely and accurate information from the drug manufacturers, heeding government regulations, and remaining as efficient as possible to serve Snyder's customers and to remain competitive. Snyder is juggling those responsibilities far more successfully today with a technology decision that has transformed its business: providing sales reps with handheld PCs running the Microsoft Windows CE operating system to disseminate and gather information. The Windows CE-based devices are being used to replace inefficient paper-based processes, and the results are dramatic. The company began a test in late 1997 and achieved full deployment in the summer of 1998. Snyder now has about 1500 representatives using NEC MobilePro 750 and MobilePro 770 handheld PCs running Windows CE and a custom pharmaceutical sales-force automation application from IMS Health Strategic Technologies. The accuracy rate for sales data collected on behalf of its customers has jumped to 100 percent, up from 85 to 90 percent with the paper-based process. Moreover, the time it takes Snyder to provide reports to its clients has dropped to 10 days after a sales call is made. Those reports used to take 60 days or longer.

"The bottom line is that we can provide far better service to our customers, which lets them make decisions faster and gives us an edge on our competition," says Tom Pollock, senior director of information systems at Snyder. "By moving to the Windows CE-based technology, we've eliminated a lot of internal headaches that we had using paper. We're making our customers happy, and we're doing that by being a lot faster and more accurate with about the same expense as the paper-based system."

SNYDER HEALTHCARE SALES SNAPSHOT

Snyder Healthcare Sales replaced its antiquated paper-based system with a sales-force automation system that delivers valuable information to its pharmaceutical clients after sales calls. The change was mandatory in order to win a bid for a large contract from a leading pharmaceutical company. The long-term benefits of this system include improved accuracy and quicker data delivery to clients. The company's knowledge-management system was built with the following products:

Operating Systems	■ Microsoft Windows CE
	■ Microsoft Windows NT Server
Hardware Products	■ NEC MobilePro 750 handheld PCs
	■ NEC MobilePro 770 handheld PCs

Problems with Paper

Snyder relied for years on paper-based *call cards* its representatives used during sales visits to physicians. The call cards were pre-printed sheets containing information such as physicians' contact information, products that were discussed with the physician, and the samples left behind in a physician's office. The U.S. Food and Drug Administration (FDA) also requires physician signatures as verification of the type and amount of drug samples left by the Snyder sales reps.

Call cards were the best method for the times, but they presented Snyder and its customers with frustrating errors and inefficiencies, Pollock says. "There were multiple copies of the call cards. One was kept by the sales rep, one by the doctor, another went to the client pharmaceutical company, while a fourth would go to an outside company that scanned the information and returned it in an electronic format for us to use for reporting," Pollock says, adding that this was common industry practice. "There was a lot of potential for errors and incomplete forms. Because the rep wrote the information by hand, the scanning company might have difficulty, for example, discerning a 7 from a 1." Snyder maintained staff to check for errors, and those workers would sometimes send call cards that had missing or incorrect information back to the reps for correction.

By the time that the whole process was finished, it took 60 days or more after the initial sales call to send the data back to the company's clients. Snyder's clients, who relied on Snyder's reports to make sales and marketing decisions, lost valuable time as a result.

Handheld Computers

The end of the paper-based sales system began the day Snyder bid for a major contract from a large pharmaceutical company, a project that promised to keep 400 Snyder sales reps busy. Snyder got the contract, partly due to its decision to upgrade its processes. "Because of the size of the client and the focus of the sales force, we needed to come up with a faster and more accurate way of gathering information," Pollock says. "We're in a competitive business, and to get this contract we had to re-evaluate our processes for tracking and disseminating information."

Snyder evaluated what kind of system would fit its needs and the needs of the client, what the rollout timeframe should be, and whether to build the system itself or buy it. The company also looked at the form-factor options, beginning with laptops—the obvious choice at first glance, because Snyder already had some laptops in the field. "We decided to go with palm-size or handheld type devices rather than laptops," Pollock says. "They are a lot cheaper to support than laptops, and they pose less risk while offering greater conveniences for sales reps. It's a lot harder to damage the hard drive or to load unauthorized software. They're smaller and easier for reps to carry in a briefcase or coat pocket, they turn on instantly instead of having to boot up, letting the reps work faster and more efficiently, and they allow for signature-capture capabilities."

That left Snyder to decide which operating system to use and how to approach the task of implementing a company standard. The first decision was quickly narrowed to Windows CE, Pollock says. "We looked at some other systems, including the Palm OS, but they simply did not have the range of functionality and features that we needed," he continues. "The Palm OS form factor was too small for what we were looking for and did not offer the range of choices in hardware that we found with Windows CE. Windows CE also offers a lot more features that can be used with sales-force automation applications, such as the pocket versions of Microsoft Excel and Microsoft Word." Windows CE also made a lot of sense because it would integrate easily with Snyder's Windows-based desktops and Windows NT Server-based back-end systems, while offering the same rich graphical interface and development environment as other Windows products.

Software Solutions

Snyder's decision to use Windows CE as its mobile operating system was sealed when the company met with representatives of IMS Health at a Microsoft-sponsored presentation on mobile computing. IMS Health, a Microsoft solution provider, is a global leader in pharmaceutical-relationship management. Many of Snyder's clients used IMS Health Strategic Technologies' suite of products for use on laptops as part of an integrated sales and marketing information system for accessing and generating information and reports. IMS Health Strategic Technologies, supporting Snyder's decision to go with the Windows CE platform, was able to offer a related product called SteppingStone for Windows CE. The product is customizable so Snyder was able to build in features that fit its specific business rules.

Evan Sohn, vice president for business development of IMS Health Strategic Technologies, says the company has issued more than 10,000 user licenses for its handheld-computing products, which are targeted to pharmaceutical salesforce automation. Of those products, nearly 40 percent are Windows CE-based, and that number is growing daily. "As a company focused on delivering strategic products to the pharmaceutical marketplace, we firmly believe that Windows CE will play a significant and growing role in helping us deliver strategic technology. The added value that it brings in terms of more functionality, more form factors, and more memory gives us the ability to deliver better products," Sohn says. "Data is the lifeblood of the pharmaceutical industry, and Windows CE helps us design technology solutions for customers that deliver not only data, but more importantly insight."

David Maurer, director of development for IMS Health Strategic Technologies, says that, from a developer's perspective, Windows CE is significantly better than alternative operating systems. "We've talked to a lot of developers and hear complaints about the limitations of the tools available for mobile computing applications," says Maurer, whose company uses the Microsoft Visual Studio development system. "From our experience, Windows CE is leaps and bounds beyond the proprietary environments we've worked in before and the limited tool sets of competing products. The tools are great, the documentation is great, and the open design environment helps us big time."

The Total Solution

Snyder's rollout plans for Windows CE include deploying its NEC MobilePro units to another 1000 sales representatives in the United States, with the possibility of expanding to another 1500 sales personnel in Europe.

The sales reps use their Windows CE-based devices for gathering the same kind of information that was collected on paper, but now the process is much faster and more efficient. Using a variety of pull-down menus, radio buttons, and other familiar Windows features, the reps can easily access or enter information on physicians, the types of drugs they typically prescribe, and samples that are left behind. The devices have a small but comfortable keyboard for entering notes following a sales call, and they also contain the call-reporting and signature-capture system designed specifically for the pharmaceutical business to use on palm-size and handheld PCs running Windows CE. Features of these systems include the following:

- **Profile Maintenance** This feature enables Snyder to add, modify, or delete accounts using its own business rules, and profiles include physician affiliations and organizations.

- **Call Reporting** All details of the call are recorded, including the products described, their order of priority, and other information associated with the sales call.

- **Sample Disbursement** During sales calls, representatives leave product (drug) samples for the physician. The SteppingStone solution for Windows CE captures all the information necessary to properly disburse a drug sample to a physician.

- **Signature Capture** This FDA-compliant function makes it easy to electronically capture the doctor's signature.

Pollock says one of the great features of the Windows CE-based devices is that the sales representatives cannot save a file after a call until all the information is recorded, including a physician's signature. This eliminates the time and expense involved in the old paper-based system of tracking down reps and asking them to enter missing information. It moves the error-correction process, Pollock says, from the back-end of the paper system to the point of entry.

At the end of each day, the Snyder sales reps log on to the company's network from the site of a local Internet service provider, using a secure dial-up connection that is made from the NEC MobilePro's modem. Once connected, the handheld PC sends the information through encrypted FTP and synchronizes the information with the back-end databases residing on a Windows NT Server-based box at an IMS Service Center. From there, the information is collated and distributed to the appropriate client pharmaceutical companies and to Snyder. Snyder is working on replicating the back-end databases to its headquarters (see Figure 4-3). Snyder plans to use SQL Server to take advantage of features such as sophisticated data-warehousing functionality, which will let Snyder provide critical business information to clients even faster and alleviate the need for paper reporting.

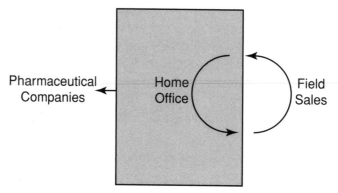

Figure 4-3. *Sales force automation.*

"This system has already gotten us positive comments from our customers, who now can get complete, accurate reports from us within 10 days after the initial sales call," Pollock says. "This lets them make faster decisions and better forecasts about their products. Before, they were looking at a 60-day delay in information, and the data would not be complete." The Snyder sales representatives using the Windows CE-based devices are also happy. "We've gotten very, very positive comments from the field reps," he says. "Our sales people are very aggressive and don't want to wait for a machine to boot up. Now with their Windows CE-based devices they simply push the 'On' button and they're working. There's no boot time, and they can accomplish a lot while waiting in a reception area or sitting in their car just before a meeting."

Pollock says Windows CE technology delivers many more benefits at roughly the same cost for what was being spent on paper-based processing. The company is now thinking ahead to future improvements to this solution and additional uses to take advantage of Windows CE. "We're looking at using the Windows CE technology in combination with the Web for gathering information and for internal processes such as updating personnel files," he says. "It's offering us many different options for improving and streamlining our business processes and tying in with other corporate business operations systems."

ONLINE CUSTOMER SUPPORT

Solutions based on handheld computers and Windows CE certainly help manage customers prior to the sale. However, if the relationship is to continue, customers also expect service after the sale. A major advantage of the Internet is that it allows more and more companies to provide that service in the form of online support. Microsoft is leading this charge with its variety of online support options. The company must provide product support to millions of customers around the world. But the most demanding users are technically savvy software developers, consultants, and resellers. Answering the questions of developers and resellers often identifies key support issues for larger customer communities.

To provide prompt, accurate technical support for these specialized audiences, Microsoft recently added a browser-based newsgroup feature to several of its main technical-information Web sites: Microsoft Developer Network (MSDN), serving developers; Microsoft Direct Access, serving consultants and resellers; and Microsoft TechNet, serving IT professionals. The sites not only answer technical questions but also feed a growing knowledge repository that gives faster answers to independent Microsoft technology providers, Microsoft support professionals, and Microsoft product-development teams. The online dialogue also fosters a greater sense of community among users and between Microsoft and its customers. These easily accessible communities already receive thousands of customer service questions a day. Ultimately, they also provide Microsoft a way to better understand problems so it can continue to improve its products.

MSDN SNAPSHOT

With the help of partner ECMS, Microsoft built a Web-based newsgroup feature for its developer support sites. The solution enables developers around the world to get help anytime they need it, often from peers, rather than clogging up the company's support lines. The company added this feature to the Microsoft Developer Network (MSDN) site, which serves developers, to Microsoft Direct Access, which serves consultants and resellers, and to Microsoft TechNet, which serves IT professionals. The solution was built on the following products:

Operating Systems	■ Microsoft Windows NT Server 4
Productivity Applications	■ Microsoft Internet Explorer 4
Development Products	■ Microsoft Visual Studio 6

continued

MSDN Snapshot *continued*

Server Products	■ Microsoft Exchange Server 5.5
	■ Microsoft Internet Information Server
	■ Active Server Pages

Easy Access to Support

On MSDN Online, the Microsoft Developer Network Web site, developers can find a broad range of technical information on Microsoft products, from operating systems to the BackOffice family and Office products. However, until recently, it was basically a one-way street: Microsoft posted information, and developers read it. Developers who needed information that wasn't on the MSDN site either had to pay for a support call to Microsoft or access an independent newsgroup service using a specialized Network News Transfer Protocol (NNTP) news client. NNTP is a widely accepted protocol for exchanging news articles, but it's difficult to use and offers no search capabilities. Microsoft wanted a Web-enabled newsgroup service that would both be accessible to many more users and also much easier to use.

Microsoft engaged Microsoft Certified Solution Provider ECMS (Enterprise Communications and Messaging Solutions) of Columbia, South Carolina, to build a Web-enabled, newsgroup interface to the MSDN and Direct Access Web sites. The solution uses an HTML user interface running on Exchange 5.5 Public Folders. Individual communities are stored in unique public folders, which are available through the HTML interface. Exchange provides a rich search capability as well as the ability to use the familiar Outlook messaging and collaboration client to manage information. HTML functionality gives greater access and connection to the knowledge repository. Finally, because Exchange already provides a set of built-in management, search, and categorization technologies, the solution was completed in just two months.

Public Discussion Groups

These Web-enabled public folders contain discussion threads on all major Microsoft products that interest developers, allowing developers to direct their questions or seek answers easily from the correct thread. The high volume of question-and-answer threads form a key source of knowledge, not only for the technology providers but also for Microsoft support professionals, who have to focus their support services and find best-practice models. The Microsoft support staff now has a new tool for identifying and monitoring threads of key interest to Microsoft customers and independent technology providers. Microsoft's support staff can now build on knowledge gained from the worldwide community of developers who work with Microsoft products to solve technical problems.

Although the company has hired staff to respond to technical questions around the clock, the Web-based community solution is a more effective, less expensive support channel than answering phone calls. Rather than waiting on the phone, users can find fast answers themselves using the knowledge repository. The newsgroups also allow Microsoft support professionals to focus their phone time on the more difficult questions that might not be addressed online. The benefit to developers, obviously, is that they get answers much faster and more easily. Says Benjamin Walvoord, an ECMS developer who worked on the project, "Microsoft and its customers are all learning together, from one another. It's like giving everyone the answers to the test so everyone does well."

The newsgroup-fed knowledge tool is also providing valuable input for product development and improvement at Microsoft. The same product-support team that handles telephone support now also monitors these newsgroups and forwards product-improvement ideas to appropriate product teams. With more than 30,000 ideas generated in the first few weeks, the online discussions are providing Microsoft developers with plenty of direction.

Knowledge Portal Features

Since the launch of the newsgroup feature on the Direct Access site in late 1998 and the MSDN Online and TechNet sites in April 1999, tens of thousands of developers have engaged in question-and-answer discussion threads. In many respects, the Microsoft support newsgroup works like any other newsgroup: users either search current postings to see if their questions have already been answered, or they post questions and wait for either a Microsoft support professional or another developer to respond. Several features, however, set the Microsoft solution apart from other news services:

- It requires a standard Web browser rather than an NNTP client, making it much easier to use.

- It offers a search capability, which allows users to zero in on their questions or answers rather than scrolling through hundreds of entries.

A subscription/personalization service allows users to subscribe to specific subjects and to be alerted when there are updates to the threads to which they have subscribed. Subscriptions and alerts add a real-time dimension to the newsgroup service and make it more responsive and relevant to users with specific interests. This frees people from having to check periodically for new messages in their interest areas. Finally, the Microsoft newsgroup is much easier to use and navigate than standard newsgroups because of its familiar Outlook and Web-browser interface.

The MSDN/Direct Access technical communities are the first fully functional Web-enabled newsgroups to run on Exchange Server. The ability of Exchange to run newsgroups, provide subscription, file attachments, and file searching functionality in a Web-based package creates an unparalleled knowledge resource. Because users tap into the newsgroup using a browser instead of a traditional NNTP newsreader, they circumvent proxy-server and firewall restrictions. Because permissions for individual users can be applied to individual public folders on Exchange servers, multiple newsgroup implementations can be deployed on the same hardware infrastructure.

Looking ahead, Microsoft and ECMS are working on tools to maintain and improve the quality of the knowledge base by enhancing the automatic indexing process and finding ways to measure quality other than by document age alone.

CORRESPONDENCE MANAGEMENT

Connect Austria markets wireless communications under the brand name ONE. With so much information available on an ongoing basis, ONE wanted to guard against overwhelming its employees with data. To head off information overload, IT managers customized the company's knowledge-management system by setting up Exchange Public Folders for groups that share responsibilities and interests. Public folders provide authorized users with a common repository for e-mail, threaded discussions, contact information, and calendars. "With Exchange, you can filter to provide users with the information they need, not just with large quantities of information," Peter Filka, IT Codirector for Connect Austria, says.

The customer-service call center is an example of how ONE uses public folders in its daily operations. When call-center employees received questions via e-mail, they would print them and deliver them to someone who could answer the question. Then that person would key the answer and send it back to the customer. To streamline this process, ONE created a correspondence-management tool that takes advantage of the company's collective knowledge and experience. Now, Outlook categorizes each question based on the presence of keywords in the e-mail and routes the message to a designated Exchange

Public Folder. Then a customer-service representative responds to the question, often with a prewritten answer. This has improved response times and freed customer-service representatives to perform other tasks. In addition, ONE managers can now track and analyze these e-mail messages, tailoring their services to meet customers' needs better.

Such responsiveness wouldn't have been possible before. With knowledge-management tools such as this correspondence-management application, ONE can transform raw information—such as customer questions—into shared knowledge that helps the company become more responsive. And the longer the system is in place, the more integral that kind of performance will be to day-to-day operations. Says Filka, "The importance of our knowledge-management system will grow day by day because the amount of information we collect grows day by day."

CONNECT AUSTRIA ONE SNAPSHOT

Connect Austria needed to provide its employees with an easy method to share information. The result is a knowledge-management solution that improves communication, facilitates knowledge sharing, and reduces sharing time. Products that Connect Austria used in its solution include the following:

Operating Systems
- Microsoft Windows NT Server
- Microsoft Windows NT Workstation

Productivity Applications
- Microsoft Office

Internet Tools
- Microsoft Internet Explorer

Server Products
- Microsoft Exchange Server
- Microsoft SNA Server
- Microsoft SQL Server
- EARIS Document Library

WRAP UP

Knowledge management helps companies better manage and support their customers. The case studies in this chapter illustrated the following points about knowledge management:

- Contact management is an important part of a knowledge-management system. It helps ensure that companies are working with timely, accurate intelligence about each of its customers.

- Microsoft uses knowledge-management systems based on Outlook and Exchange to support its sales representatives as well as its customers.

- Knowledge management is more than sales-force automation. An effective knowledge-management system also completes the information loops by returning customer feedback to sales, marketing, and manufacturing.

- Knowledge-management systems that use handheld devices to replace paper remove error and delays from sales and data-collection processes.

- The case studies in this chapter illustrated how quickly and easily most businesses can build knowledge-management systems using Outlook and Exchange.

Taking Stock

1. Does your sales force have the information it needs in order to be successful? Is that information accurate and current?

2. Is your company still using paper-based sales processes?

3. Does your company have a mechanism to return customer feedback to your sales, marketing, and manufacturing departments? How well does it work?

4. Does your company frequently drop orders or ship orders late?

5. Are your manufacturing and marketing departments working with accurate sales numbers in order to produce an appropriate amount of product?

6. Do you support your customers online?

7. When customers correspond with your company, is that correspondence tracked?

ACTION PLAN

❏ Implement a knowledge-management system that helps your sales force work with more timely and accurate information.

❏ Make intelligence from the sales department available to other departments, such as marketing and manufacturing.

❏ Build an online knowledge base to support your company's customers.

❏ Implement tracking systems that help ensure customers are pleased with the results of any correspondence they have with your company.

Chapter 5

Employee Management

Think of knowledge management as customer service for your employees, helping them become happier, smarter, and more productive in their roles.

Few companies can say that their employees are not their most valuable assets; knowledge management can help every company take better care of its employees. With an effective knowledge-management solution, companies can better motivate their employees, better reward them, and align their skills with corporate needs.

Effective knowledge-management solutions deliver training, track employees' skills and competencies, remove barriers to productivity, provide current company information, manage benefits, help supervisors staff their departments, and simplify expense reimbursement. Dynamic market conditions can catch companies without valuable skill sets across its employees, for example. Knowledge-management systems can identify skill gaps as well as provide mechanisms for closing those gaps. Identifying employees that significantly outperform their peers is useful for finding best practices that companies can share with other employees.

Employee management is thus an ideal area for companies to improve with knowledge-management solutions. This chapter describes how some companies, including Microsoft, address the issues you've just read about.

TRAINING

Training is an obvious target for knowledge management. Connect Austria is a prime example of a company that relies on its system for orienting the employees it hires. Training 50 to 100 new hires a month quickly and keeping veteran employees up to date on new policies and procedures remains a top priority for managers at this company. Thanks to the company's knowledge-management system, new employees can ramp up more quickly than before. According to Peter Filka, IT Codirector for Connect Austria, the average person takes less than half an hour to learn how to use the system.

For training and company information, new and veteran employees find the corporate intranet a valuable part of the knowledge-management system. Connect Austria publishes its handbooks, manuals, and other administrative information on its intranet. While knowledge-management systems won't replace existing training materials, they do make those training materials more available to users. Using the system's search tool, employees can find information they need quickly. Whenever managers approve a change, they notify employees by e-mail. By publishing this kind of information to its intranet, the company saves both the time and the fixed costs associated with frequently printing and distributing thousands of memos and handbooks.

SKILL ALIGNMENT

Training to keep employees' skills current is only half the story, though; effective solutions also help companies align employees' skills with the companies' needs. For example, Siemens' 400,000 employees make it the fourth largest company in the world and a leader in highly complex SAP R/3 implementation. Siemens Business Services division has 1600 SAP R/3 consultants working around the globe to provide customers with solutions to complex business and technical problems. For Siemens, the key to managing such a geographically dispersed workforce was to create Consultant Network.

Consultant Network includes a resource-planning tool that helps Siemens track its experts and assign them to projects worldwide. Illustrated in Figure 5-1, this tool gives the company an easy way to profile consultants, identify expert skills, and look up availability so that it can assign the right person to the right job at the right time. "In the consulting business, changes can happen very quickly," says Martin Luckfiel, KM Solution Manager for Siemens. "A project may be delayed unexpectedly, causing us to shift our resources. A customer in London is expecting a consultant with certain skills to show up next week, while the assigned consultant has been delayed in Malaysia for two weeks. Using our resource planning tool, we can zero in on all consultants who have the right qualifications and availability to get the job done."

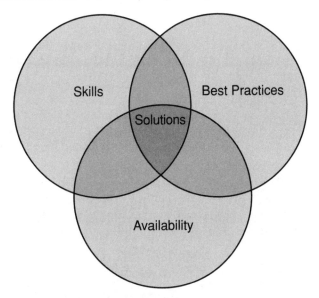

Figure 5-1. *Consultant Network.*

Consultant Network enables Siemens' consultants to find answers and best practices faster than they could previously. "Customers expect fast, professional responses," Luckfiel says. "This knowledge base gives us the ultimate competitive advantage by enabling us to provide that fast, accurate response. A customer knows they can't get our five best people assigned to their project; but this system lets us leverage all our best consultants for every assignment. The sharing of expertise lets our junior consultants be almost as smart and productive as our senior consultants. Customers really appreciate this."

Siemens' knowledge-management system has enough flexibility and scalability to meet the company's continually growing business needs and to stay a step ahead of the competition. According to Luckfiel, "The knowledge-management solution has had quite an impact on our company, and people see this system as a real aid to their daily work. The technology makes people eager to collaborate, and its accessibility allows everyone to stay up to date on every customer. The Consultant Network has truly become our digital nervous system. It's the backbone of our business, giving us a major competitive advantage."

BENEFITS

Microsoft is leading the knowledge-management charge. In my conversations with the company's employees, they always rave about how easy it is to work with human resources through its knowledge-management portals. They also tell me how little paper they have to use to process forms such as vacation requests. Before delving into that, however, a bit of background is appropriate. Microsoft is well known for hiring smart, highly productive people who are focused on developing top-quality products, programs, and services. To help keep employees enthusiastic and dedicated, the company offers a variety of benefits, including stock options, a stock-purchasing program, comprehensive health insurance, and a 401(k) program.

In the past decade, Microsoft has grown from fewer than 10,000 employees to more than 20,000. This rapid growth contributed to a complex benefits package, which increased the number of paper and e-mail forms employees were required to use to enroll for and manage their benefits. Additionally, all human-resources materials—including benefits information, enrollment forms, and time cards—were scattered throughout the company's servers and buildings. This lack of centralized information made it difficult for employees to find what they needed quickly and distracted them from their work. Employees needed an easy way to access this information, to personalize and update their records, and to check the status of their benefits. To solve this problem, the Human Resources (HR) department faced the challenge of developing an intranet site that offered one-stop shopping for all its information and processes. "Our goal with an HR intranet is to provide excellent customer service to Microsoft employees, so that they can focus on getting their jobs done," says Kimberly Mecham, product manager for HR Operations. "They need easy access to information, and they need to be able to get that information from anywhere at any time."

In October 1995, Microsoft's HR group introduced HR Web, an intranet site that serves as the foundation for a growing number of specialized applications. These applications include information about and enrollment for stock options, employee stock purchase discounts, a 401(k) plan, and absence reporting. Additionally, the site hosts a wide variety of employee-related publications, including the employee handbook, a weekly newsletter, and campus maps. Employees also enjoy visiting one site to learn about commuting options, vacation travel packages, tuition assistance, and community-volunteer opportunities.

HR Web is available seven days a week, 24 hours a day so that employees can access information and forms from any location—at home, while traveling, or at work—when they need it. This flexibility frees them up from having to come to the office to retrieve paper forms. The environment is personalized and secure so that an employee can check how many stock options she's vested, how many vacation days she's used, and if her medical insurance will cover a particular ailment—all in less than five minutes. The employee data in the site—including name, social security number, manager, hire date, and employment status—flows from Microsoft's SAP HR module, eliminating the need for someone to enter the data more than once. This process also ensures that the data is current.

Since its inception, HR Web has saved Microsoft more than $1 million a year, and it has eliminated more than 200 paper forms. More than 21,000 users access the site each month, which has helped eliminate the need to retain nine people just for answering e-mail and phone requests. The company is saving 75 to 90 percent in postage and material costs. The following sections tell you more about how Microsoft realized these terrific gains.

Paperless Management

HR Web simplifies the process for reporting vacation time, sick time, and, for hourly employees, work time with a time-card/absence-reporting application. This application can determine if an employee is hourly or salaried and direct him to time cards or absence-reporting forms accordingly. It can also calculate how many vacation hours an employee has left, based on how many he has already used. It replaces a paper-based time-card system and an e-mail-based absence-reporting system, decreasing processing time by half.

Payroll and Direct Deposit

The payroll area of HR Web includes an online direct-deposit feature that enables employees to specify how they want to allocate their paychecks to a selected bank, investment accounts, and personal benefits. Additionally, HR Web posts earnings statements for each employee to view in a secure environment. This has eliminated the need to print and mail paychecks or paystubs, saving the company $600,000 a year.

Stock Purchase Programs

Microsoft's Employee Stock Purchase Plan (ESPP) enables employees to buy Microsoft stock at a discount. Prior to HR Web's ESPP application, HR sent a record of individual stock purchases to each participating employee who requested one. These records, which include the total number of shares an employee has purchased along with the purchase price, had to be downloaded from the company's source system, printed, and distributed. In addition, HR sent a memo to notify employees of their purchases after each six-month purchase period.

Now, using HR Web's ESPP intranet application, each employee can access a view-only page that provides a record of her stock-purchase history. Employees can also use the ESPP application to enroll in or withdraw from the program, receiving a full refund on their contributions at any time. In addition to providing these services, the ESPP application houses a real-time Microsoft stock ticker, Microsoft's stock-split history, and information that helps employees navigate tax-related issues. By channeling the employee stock-purchase program onto the intranet, HR has eliminated paper and e-mail enrollment forms, reducing administrative costs dramatically. Materials and postage expenses have dropped 75 percent, and e-mail volume resulting from employee questions has decreased 25 percent.

Like the ESPP application, the stock-option application provides an individual account of each employee's stock-option history. It indicates how many options an employee has been granted, how many options that employee has vested, how many he has exercised, and how many are left to exercise. HR uses this application to distribute stock-option grants upon hire or after a review period and to confirm when an employee exercises options. Before this tool was available, a stock administrator spent more than four hours each day sending individual e-mail summaries to employees who requested the information. Now it takes an administrator no more than an hour a day to answer stock-related questions. HR also eliminated the need to hire three temporary employees during each review period to distribute grant packages. Now packets are ready for distribution in only eight hours, versus three weeks, and only one full-time employee is involved in the process. Finally, HR has reduced the time required to distribute exercise confirmations (from 15 hours to five hours a week), and the department no longer needs to store paper records of employee stock transactions because the records are all online.

401(k) Administration

Microsoft offers all salaried employees a 401(k) plan and matches their contributions up to a certain amount. The plan is administered by an investment firm, which manages a variety of top-rated mutual funds, as well as other investment vehicles, from which employees can choose to invest their money. With HR Web's 401(k) application, employees can enroll in the plan, choose investment options, and change the percentage of eligible compensation they want to contribute to the plan. The application provides detailed information on different funds and a link to the investment firm's home page, where employees can reallocate their contributions. After an employee signs up for the 401(k) plan, the application automatically notifies the investment firm and the Microsoft payroll department, eradicating the need for human intervention.

STAFFING

Small organizations can be nimble. They are often quick to reorganize and reconfigure in response to escalating competition, demanding customers, and changes in market conditions. Because of these abilities, they are frequently well positioned to take advantage of new and emerging market opportunities. If they change effectively, they are more likely to prosper and grow larger to build on their successes. But there lies one of the major challenges to all successful companies: a larger organization is rarely as nimble as it was in its early days, yet its need to respond promptly to changes and opportunities remains unchanged.

This was the challenge the Microsoft HR department faced. The company's success had resulted in an explosive growth in personnel, as noted earlier. However, this rapid growth made it significantly more difficult to manage staffing issues throughout the company. Each of the company's business units had its own system for tracking and managing headcount. When managers changed their teams, they initiated a paper-based transaction to update the corporate records. Managers would submit updates to HR personnel, who maintained 18 databases located worldwide. Twice a week, these 18 databases were consolidated into one reporting database. By the time the information was consolidated, it was at least four days behind reality.

Such a complex set of systems and processes did not lend itself well to rapidly transferring information, which is what managers needed to do to make effective staffing decisions. The information in the central reporting database was useful to corporate HR and Finance for quarterly and annual closing information; however, it was of virtually no use to the business-unit managers because they had no way to access it. That compromised the abilities of managers to change their organizations quickly in response to rising business challenges.

Tracking Headcount

To solve these problems, Microsoft installed SAP R/3's HR module to consolidate the 18 HR databases and developed an intranet-based application called HeadTrax. HeadTrax provides Microsoft employees throughout the world with Web access to headcount information for the entire organization. Both SAP and Microsoft's domestic recruiting database download data into the HeadTrax database every night, ensuring that the information in HeadTrax is current.

HeadTrax is particularly useful to managers who need to view and change their organizations rapidly. Managers can view employees by cost center or by their positions in the organizational hierarchy. HeadTrax also enables managers to look at headcount information in different timeframes for planning purposes.

They can view data from the preceding business day, data that is effective as of the end of the fiscal month, or all open positions before the end of the fiscal year. HeadTrax also lets managers query organizational data—for example, finding all employees with a specific job title attached to a specific organization. This feature provides them with a wealth of accurate, up-to-date information that was difficult, if not impossible, to get by using the previous system.

HeadTrax not only makes it easy for managers to draw current information from a global database, but it also provides managers and other employees with an easy-to-use, paperless system for entering and updating information. HeadTrax enables managers (and administrative assistants working on their behalf) to view and update data, making it simple for an assistant to process an employee transfer or initiate a request for a contingent staff position. In addition to increasing data accuracy and detail, HeadTrax increases the finance department's visibility into the details that drive its headcount reports. HeadTrax reduces the workload for HR administrators because headcount information entered on the intranet is automatically uploaded into Microsoft's SAP HR module within one day. This represents a 300-plus percent improvement from when it took three or more days to manually reenter the information into SAP. Moreover, because the data is entered on the intranet and automatically sent to SAP, it is subject to significantly fewer of the typing errors that plagued the paper-based system. To ensure accountability, HeadTrax provides a complete audit trail for every transaction.

Managing Headcount

With more than 20,000 employees worldwide, HeadTrax has dramatically changed how Microsoft manages headcount. Those changes enable managers to respond more quickly to opportunities in the marketplace. HeadTrax processes approximately 24,000 employee transactions per month, which is a boon to the growing organization. Prior to HeadTrax, the task of collecting and processing headcount-change data was so time intensive that only 10,000 transactions per year could be completed. This represents a significant improvement in the throughput of information for such a rapidly growing company.

For Microsoft, HeadTrax ensures the easy access to accurate information about their organizations that managers need. It is decreasing the costs and increasing the efficiency of Microsoft's HR and Finance departments, which own the person and position information, respectively. These departments have replaced the 18 HR databases and all the business-unit systems with one effective application that works for everybody. HeadTrax improves data integrity throughout the company by providing a single repository for global headcount information. Future versions of HeadTrax will do even more. They will enable designated users to initiate recruitment for an employee position, to create and post job descriptions on Microsoft's intranet and on the Web, and to model their organizations in different ways without having to save each version in the SAP HR module.

This ability to reshape the organization quickly to respond to new opportunities and new market conditions is a requirement in today's fast-paced business world. HeadTrax helps ensure that Microsoft is nimble enough to spring when opportunities present themselves.

PERFORMANCE REVIEWS

Technology will never replace a personal, face-to-face performance review, but knowledge management can make establishing and recording the review information more efficient. At Microsoft, some 3,000 managers conduct performance reviews for more than 20,000 eligible employees. The process of evaluating, updating, and managing review information has been enhanced by a desktop application used around the world: MS Review.

Managers and employees discuss performance plans and goals year-round in an ongoing process that encourages frequent communication and feedback. Twice a year, most employees participate in a comprehensive performance review. The Microsoft process for reviewing performance provides a structured method for managers and employees to set goals, review achievements, and develop an action plan for professional development. During the biannual performance-review periods, managers assign numerical performance ratings for each employee and might adjust employee compensation as a result. To help administer the biannual performance reviews, Microsoft managers rely on MS Review to see what review scores employees earned in previous periods and to enter information for the current period. They can also use MS Review to see whether the review decisions they made fall within corporate guidelines. For mid-level and senior managers, this information is particularly useful; it shows them the aggregate amounts determined by all managers within their organization and allows them to compare their numbers against their overall compensation budgets. If a particular business unit exceeds its budget, the senior manager can push the review set back to the responsible managers for reconsideration.

"MS Review isn't a tool to help managers write performance reviews," says Debbie Hickox, the product manager for MS Review. "All Microsoft employees and managers use a Microsoft Word template to prepare a summary document. Once the reviews are written, managers use MS Review to add employee review details, including a numerical performance rating, and consolidate information on employees in their organization. MS Review enables managers to analyze statistics, view budgets, and track their numbers against corporate or subsidiary budgets. It's a kind of one-stop shopping experience—providing managers with a single place where they can enter and view review details and compensation information."

Out with the Old

Prior to MS Review, the task of collecting and managing the data required for the review process was labor intensive and time consuming. Microsoft's HR group used to rely on Microsoft Excel spreadsheets to gather review information from managers. The spreadsheets grew more sophisticated, but the method for gathering and processing review information remained constant. Managers had to send the spreadsheets back to Microsoft HR, where the information would be consolidated by hand from the multitude of files. HR would roll up information for individual groups into larger group statistics, and it would then roll that information into still larger organizational information. The aggregate information could then be sent to Microsoft senior managers, who could see whether the amounts fit within the budget.

The problems associated with this method were apparent. To begin with, Microsoft did not have a centralized HR information system. Microsoft's domestic operations were handled by an HR department based in Redmond, while each subsidiary operated its own HR department and system. No system consolidated data across the entire company. HR managers could manually consolidate information from each group and subsidiary to create a corporate-wide picture; however, it was difficult to ensure that the overall view was accurate due to the possibility of human error from any point of data entry.

Moreover, managing so many files required a great deal of time. From the day HR began to develop and distribute the spreadsheet templates to the day the final information was entered into the HR systems was a full six months— and then it was time to begin the process all over again.

In with the New

Today, the review process takes about two months. Company-wide reviews still take place twice each year, but a variety of changes at Microsoft have streamlined the process considerably. Microsoft now uses the HR module of SAP R/3 to manage employee records for all its operations, domestic and international. Prior to each of the review periods, Microsoft HR extracts employee performance information from the SAP database and creates a data mart running on Microsoft SQL Server. This information serves as the core database for the review process.

Microsoft HR managers then send an e-mail message to managers of the other departments. Not only does the message remind them that it is time to do performance reviews, but it also provides a link that enables the manager to install the latest version of MS Review. When the manager logs onto the intranet and launches the application, MS Review encrypts and downloads the corresponding employee information to the manager's system. The data is then stored securely on the manager's workstation while the review period is underway.

When the time comes to make compensation decisions, managers can use MS Review to see the employee's past compensation and review ratings. They can then compare that information to other employees in the group. MS Review informs a manager precisely where an employee's salary falls relative to the recommended salary range for his position. It provides current information on performance-review ratings and an account of the number of employees who have received certain performance ratings. It even provides budget information for different compensation elements, for example, salary increases and bonuses. As the manager makes review recommendations, she enters that information into MS Review. As soon as that information has been entered and accepted in MS Review, the application transfers that information from the manager's desktop to the HR database. When an individual manager has completed her reviews, the manger then approves the entire review package by clicking a button in MS Review. At that time, MS Review notifies that manager's manager by e-mail that a set of reviews is complete and ready for examination.

Executives at the top of each organization determine how far down the management chain the MS Review tool is pushed, and they can designate certain access levels for individual managers in the hierarchy. Senior managers can use MS Review to record the information for their direct reports; they can also use MS Review's tools for real-time analysis to see how the performance review scores and compensation budgets are being distributed. "I really like the MS Review tool. I used the Excel spreadsheet review models previously, and this is a vast improvement," says Sabina Nawaz, a group program manager in HR Management and Leadership Development. "The statistical reporting lets me track employee to employee how I'm doing against my budget and other review guidelines. There are great ways to sort the data as well as see employee detail and history. MS Review is a tool that makes my job a lot easier."

After a manager has approved the review recommendations for her organization, the recommendations are passed up the managerial chain for further approvals. Mid-level and senior managers can view and modify recommendations for individual scores. If a senior manager discovers that one of his direct reports has exceeded a budget, for instance, he can send the entire set of recommendations back to that report for reconsideration. Ultimately, all the data for each group is approved by the department's top-level managers. From there, it is passed from the MS Review database to SAP R/3, where the information is linked to the employee record in the HR module. Three months later, HR personnel download all employee records to the data mart again, as the review process begins anew.

For Microsoft, MS Review is a streamlined solution that maximizes the efficiency with which managers can record their evaluations of employee performance. It provides managers throughout the organization with timely, accurate information and enables the company to manage its budgets with a higher level of effectiveness. It has cut in half the amount of time HR personnel must spend preparing materials for each review period. This frees them up to work more closely with organizational managers on other aspects of employee management. MS Review provides better information for better decisions, and that enables Microsoft managers to run their organizations more effectively.

EXPENSE MANAGEMENT

Microsoft has subsidiaries in more than 60 countries around the world. Because it has a strong worldwide presence, employees spend nearly $200 million a year traveling on business. Additionally, they often spend out-of-pocket money on work-related expenses such as meals, supplies, and entertainment. Because Microsoft is a fast-paced, dynamic work environment where employees manage a large workload, people don't want to spend a lot of time filling out expense reports. If they find time, they want to be able to submit expense-reimbursement reports easily and to be reimbursed promptly.

This was not possible with the previous system, which was based on paper forms. When employees filled out expense reports, they often did so at work because the forms were located in the office. An alternative was to complete one of many templates based on Excel. The employee then printed the reports, attached the receipts, and submitted the package to her manager, who often took longer than a week to approve it and send it on to Accounts Payable. After the form was approved, Accounts Payable would enter the information manually from the paper form into the financial system, which would issue the check. On average, this procedure could take up to three weeks, often putting employees behind on paying their bills for corporate credit cards. "Employees wanted to be reimbursed faster," explains Clayton Fleming, director at CPG Process Design. "Our challenge was to figure out how to repay them in a timely fashion without hiring more people in Accounts Payable."

Another problem was that department-specific versions of the expense-report template had been created throughout the company. At one point, 136 expense-report templates resided on various servers. The multiplicity of forms slowed processing in Accounts Payable because form processors had to standardize data from different formats. Also, outdated forms often had old account codes, obsolete mileage rates, or incorrect or missing classifications, such as airfare and entertainment expenses. These issues posed a problem for the Corporate Procurement Group (CPG), which oversees Accounts Payable.

To solve these problems, CPG developed MS Expense, an expense-reporting application that links directly with Microsoft's SAP R/3 financial module. After an employee fills out and submits an expense report over the intranet, it's automatically parked, pending management approval, in the SAP module without any manual uploading or dual entry. The employee's manager automatically receives an e-mail message that the report is ready for review. If the manager approves the expense report, the report's status changes to *Posted* in the SAP module. At this point, the report is ready for payment, which the SAP module does. Because all these steps directly create and update transactions in SAP, no manual processing is required. The automated procedure thus cuts costs, shortens the payment cycle, and eliminates data-entry errors.

An average of 15,000 Microsoft employees use MS Expense in 29 countries to process 2600 Microsoft expense reports each week. MS Expense has greatly improved Microsoft's expense-reporting function, saving the company significant sums of money and hours of work while eliminating errors that occur when processing paper forms. It saves Microsoft approximately $400,000 a year in personnel costs alone, because CPG was able to re-deploy half of its expense-reporting group to other positions. Only four people manage the expense reporting and audit processes, and CPG expects that number to diminish even further. MS Expense has also improved employee satisfaction with the expense-reimbursement process. Employees get paid in three days, not three weeks, and they can report expenses at any time from anywhere in the world.

WRAP UP

Knowledge management can help companies save significant sums of money by enabling them to improve employee management. Key areas in which knowledge management is most effective for this include the following:

- **Training helps keep employees sharp.** It can take many forms, including multimedia, online handbooks and manuals, and so on.

■ **Skill alignment ensures that the right people are working on the right projects at the right time.** Knowledge management enables companies to find experts that are available for a particular job.

■ **Benefits management is a natural target for any knowledge-management system.** Companies can simplify paper-based systems, reduce HR costs, provide corporate information to employees, and more.

■ **Bigger companies can benefit most from better staffing management.** Using knowledge management, those companies can keep track of headcount and reorganize more quickly.

■ **Performance reviews, as demonstrated by MS Review, are more efficient when moved from manual processes to knowledge-management systems.** As a result, reviews are completed on time, and supervisors can better manage their budgeting processes.

■ **Expense reimbursement is best done on an intranet.** Companies can significantly reduce the cost and turn-around time for reimbursing employees for out-of-pocket expenses, improving morale and productivity.

Taking Stock

1. Are your HR processes automated as much as they could be?

2. Do your employees grumble about your HR processes?

3. Do your employees receive the training required to perform their jobs the way you'd like?

4. Do your employees have available training for the skills that might be required as the business climate and other pressures change?

5. Do you know who the experts are in your organization? Can managers in your company quickly identify the right people to assign to a particular project and determine their availability?

6. Does your organization use paper-based forms for vacation requests, benefit-enrollment forms, and other HR information?

7. Can your employees view relevant HR information about themselves on your intranet?

8. Would your company be able to reorganize or move staff around quickly?

9. Do you view your performance review process positively or negatively?

10. Do you submit expenses using paper-based forms? How long does it take for employees to get expense checks after submitting forms?

ACTION PLAN

❑   Identify the various sources of HR data that exist in your organization.

❑   Identify the key HR processes that would benefit most from online automation.

❑   Walk the halls and talk to employees to get a better feel for the types of problems a knowledge-management system might solve, as well as opportunities it might seize.

Chapter 6

Business Planning

Enable your company's knowledge workers to make better decisions by providing them with more complete information on which to act.

Constantly changing business climates challenge businesses to revise their strategies within every area of the company. Strategies change from supply rooms to executive suites. As a result, companies are embracing the idea that they must share information across all levels and empower knowledge workers with decision-making authority. Knowledge management supports this idea by enabling systematic access to the business data, the competitive information, and the market demographics that support decision-making processes.

All the case studies you read about in this chapter have certain things in common. By providing better access to business data and information, the knowledge-management systems of the companies profiled help employees discover trends, reduce response times, and improve competitive awareness. In short, the systems help knowledge workers in those organizations act on more complete information. Technologies that enable these results include the analysis and collaboration tools you learn about in Chapter 8, "Exchange Web Storage System."

DECISION MAKING

California Pizza Kitchen's (CPK) information systems used to run on more platforms than there were people in the IT organization. The company also had a variety of disconnected systems within its headquarters and stores. Getting timely ad hoc reports to executives, analysts, and store managers was virtually impossible because data was locked in different operational systems at different sites. CPK managers and executives, for example, wanted to know how the company was performing—which restaurants were doing well, which ones weren't, and what the company's financial picture was on a daily, even hourly, basis. The company's AS/400 held all the financial accounting records and captured daily sales data from each of the 70 stores. However, the data was captured nightly on a whole-day basis, leaving management in the dark about what was happening in restaurants at different times of the day or with different menu items. What item was selling best at lunch versus dinner? Who ordered it? How were customers paying for their meals? Analysts were expending "horrendous efforts," says Kevin Moon, director of information services at CPK, to wrestle data from one system into another for analysis. "We had lots of good data but no information. We decided to develop a data warehouse to centralize and simplify our access to business information."

CPK built its data warehouse by using Microsoft SQL Server. Hummingbird BI/Query, an enterprise-strength query and reporting tool, provides access to the data. BI/Query is part of the Hummingbird BI/Suite, a fully integrated, scalable enterprise business-intelligence solution that allows users to access and analyze information both on the desktop and over the Web. CPK chose BI/Query because of its ease of use. "BI/Query beat all the other business intelligence tools we looked at," Moon says. "In 15 minutes, users can get a handle on its basic functionality and be on their way. From there, it's easy for them to work among themselves and train one another."

CPK's data warehouse contains sales data, food-cost data, labor data, and marketing information. All of it is more granular. CPK managers and analysts use it to monitor virtually every aspect of the company's business (see Figure 6-1). For instance, analysts receive daily data from each restaurant and use BI/Query to discover which food and beverage items are selling and which ones aren't. The analysts can access incredibly detailed transactional information, such as which items sold in which service areas of a restaurant (dining room, delivery, or takeout), customer-check information (size of bill, size of party), and how many customers paid for their meals using credit cards instead of cash. Also available is labor data—how many employees worked in each job class, whether the total hours worked corresponded to the maximum allowed by company standards, and other information. Operations managers use such data to make fair comparisons of a restaurant's performance relative to other CPK restaurants of similar size and location. Finance and accounting people use the data for countless reports and analysis. "If IT staff had to generate the data for all those reports, we'd need at least two more experienced people to do it," Moon says. "With BI/Query, the work is pushed to the user where it should be."

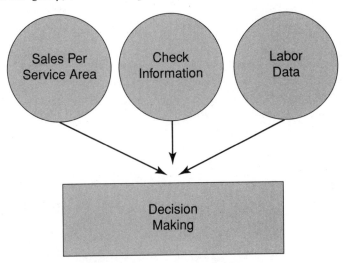

Figure 6-1. *Better decision making via business intelligence.*

CALIFORNIA PIZZA KITCHEN SNAPSHOT

California Pizza Kitchen signed Cotelligent to help it deploy a centralized data warehouse that provides faster access to data. The bottom line is that California Pizza Kitchen wanted their managers to make faster, better decisions and improve customer service by leaving their store managers free to talk face-to-face with customers. Their solution included a full range of Microsoft and non-Microsoft products:

Operating Systems	■ Microsoft Windows 95
	■ Microsoft Windows NT Server 4
Productivity Applications	■ Microsoft Office
	■ Hummingbird BI/Query
Development Tools	■ Microsoft Visual Studio 6

continued

California Pizza Kitchen Snapshot *continued*

Server Products	■ Microsoft Exchange Server
	■ Microsoft SQL Server version 6.5 (and soon 7)
	■ Microsoft Internet Information Server

Better Decisions

Because decision makers can easily access data themselves, they can generate financial and other business reports quickly and make decisions faster. According to Moon, BI/Query has made CPK's decision-making process faster and more efficient because reports that once took weeks for the information-services staff to prepare now take minutes. Analysts spend less time hunting and gathering data and more time analyzing it.

Decisions are also smarter. "Before, our promotional, marketing, and analyst employees were pretty much shooting from the hip," Moon says. "Managers had an idea of what was happening in the field, but there were no facts to back up their hunches. This data warehouse gives our knowledge workers the hard data to either support their hunches or shoot holes in them. Operating from facts saves a lot of time and a lot of poor decisions."

And CPK wants employees to value their customers, not data and systems. "We want our customers to enjoy not only great food but great atmosphere and great service," Moon explains. "To achieve great service, we want our restaurant managers and staff spending less time in the back room fussing with computer reports and more time out front with customers. We don't want to put any tools in the field that detract from customer service."

Faster Reactions

CPK's data warehouse is giving the company timely, accurate information on all of its operations. This gives the company the ability to react much faster if something's not working. The company can quickly spot changes in spending and buying patterns and make changes. "Without this ability to analyze and act on your data nearly instantaneously, you just can't catch this stuff, which means you lose money longer," says Moon.

The data warehouse has served as an impetus to integrate all the company's systems: promotional, food costing, financial. Even the company's help-desk application will soon be running on SQL Server and will be integrated with other core business systems to some degree. With so much corporate information integrated, all decision makers will be looking at the same numbers and making decisions based on fresh, accurate, consistent data. That helps everyone in the company pull together rather than work at odds with one another. "All our smart people get smarter, and our junior people benefit from the intelligence of our best people," says Moon.

TREND ANALYSIS

In the spring of 1997, when HarperCollins Publishers published *Underboss* by Peter Maas, bookstores went nuts. They all wanted stacks of the Mafia intrigue story that had received lots of media hype and was quickly followed by a TV movie. But HarperCollins was wary. In the book business, unsold product is returned at tremendous expense to the publisher. To make sure dealers were ordering only as much as they could sell, HarperCollins used a data-warehouse application called DataTracker, which runs on SQL Server, to analyze daily sales data. The publisher was able to monitor sales, regulate the flow of books into the dealer pipeline, and keep returns to an absolute minimum. Consequently, it turned a title that could have been vastly over-ordered and over-returned into a very profitable winner.

Like the music industry, the book business depends on *hits*: a hot title will often take off in a hurry, peak in six to eight weeks, and then trail off to almost nothing. The publisher has to get to market with the right number of books and get out without leaving a trail of unsold copies. Unsold books are returned at nearly the full purchase price, eating up what little profit the publisher may have made. Industry-wide, return rates run at a profit-pounding 30 percent. HarperCollins' objective, in creating a sales-tracking data warehouse several years ago, was to get that return rate down, at first into the 20 percent range, and then hopefully into the teens.

To get return rates down, you have to keep a close eye on what's selling and what's not. That isn't always easy, because the industry has traditionally focused on producing lots of titles and pushing them from warehouse to store. There was little time spent determining whether those titles were making money. "A small number of titles carry most publishers," explains Lyle Anderson, chief information officer at HarperCollins. "The trick is to know which titles are the gold mines and which are the black holes. For the former, we want to be able to print lots and sell them quickly. For the titles that bomb, we want to cut our losses and get out as soon as possible." If you're going to sell 600,000 copies of a book in just a few weeks and then sink back to zero, you have to have just-in-time sales information. And everyone in the company needs it: sales, marketing, finance, publishing, management, distribution, and other areas.

Simplicity Makes It Real

The problem with HarperCollins' previous sales-tracking data warehouse was that it was too slow, too inflexible, and too disjointed to make that information available. The data warehouse resided on a Tandem mainframe and was updated through two AS/400 computers. Even with that entire horsepower, it took two or three days to churn through 90 gigabytes of sales data, making it impractical for doing ad hoc, drill-down queries. Sales data was spread over at least three platforms, resulting in frequent data disagreement. If management, marketing, and publishing asked, "Who was our most profitable customer this month?" they were likely to get three different answers. Plus, mid-range systems were becoming too expensive. Not only were hardware and software costs soaring, but development costs were soaring, too.

The consistency and simplicity of the Microsoft platform held great appeal for HarperCollins, which was feeling the cost and cumbersome weight of a heterogeneous environment. "We were looking to simplify our world," Anderson explains. "The old sales-tracking data warehouse was expensive and complex; we just didn't have the technical expertise to manage it. We had to have something less expensive to help with our profitability. And we had to have something faster."

HarperCollins decided to move its data warehouse and online analytical processing (OLAP) solution to the Microsoft platform. With SQL Server storing and fetching information on the back end and Microsoft desktop tools—Microsoft Excel, Microsoft Access, and Microsoft Internet Explorer browser software—delivering it on the front end, HarperCollins entered into a whole new realm of business intelligence. Knowledge workers throughout the company now have fast, easy access to sales, inventory, and return data on all HarperCollins titles. They can drill down to title, type of book (business, self-help, and so forth), customer, month, week, or any other variable to find out the answers to questions such as the following: What was our profitability on this title this week with this customer? Is our marketing program giving us the results we expected? Which categories are our strongest sellers this quarter?

Making Informed Decisions

A HarperCollins financial analyst might see a drop in profitability at month's end. Using DataTracker, he can slice down and trace the profitability dip to business books. He can hone in on hardback or paperback, isolate a certain category of books, and then drill all the way down to the problem titles. "We just couldn't pick this needle out of the haystack before," explains Stuart Mowat, director of decision support systems at HarperCollins. "Once we find the problem, we can adjust the supply chain accordingly, perhaps canceling a reprint. We can look at point-of-sale data to see if something bigger is happening in the division as a whole. Analysts, sales people, editors, and management are asking these kinds of questions all the time, allowing us to use data in a very proactive fashion to impact our profitability. It's given an awful lot of power to an awful lot of people throughout the enterprise."

HarperCollins sales representatives visit customers like B. Dalton and Borders with laptops and DataTracker in hand. They pull up the customer's orders and show them what they're selling and what they aren't, which can help customers make decisions about what they should buy based on current trends and their order histories. By helping customers order books that will sell, HarperCollins reduces returns and thus improves its bottom line.

Predicting the Future

Forecasting is a hot new capability delivered by DataTracker on SQL Server. HarperCollins has long captured historical sales and return data. However, the SQL Server-based solution allows the company to analyze that historical data a lot more cost effectively, and the application can also capture current sales data. Combined with the historical data, the sales data lets the company forecast sales of specific titles.

HarperCollins is bringing its general ledger data into DataTracker, adding actual profitability data to the mix. It is also building a SQL Server database to analyze point-of-sale data to see how specific titles are moving through the market. If the company knows how one product is moving through the channel, it can get a feel for how other titles might move. Best of all, says Mowat, the DataTracker/SQL Server solution gives HarperCollins a single version of the truth. "Companies will pay a lot of money for that. Our data warehouse on a common, accessible platform ensures that everyone in the company is operating from the same set of data. Decisions are consistent and trackable. When someone asks, 'Who is our most profitable customer?' everyone gets the same answer."

Results in the Pudding

HarperCollins' Microsoft-based data warehouse is showing benefits in several other areas. The first is speed. SQL Server query response times are at least 10 times faster than the previous Tandem-AS/400 solution, returning results in two or three hours rather than two or three days. Overnight run time went down by a third—from six hours to four. That means more questions get asked, more decisions get made, and more work gets done every day. Anderson says he was teased by colleagues when first considering SQL Server for his large data warehouse. "It's a toy, they told us, unsuitable for data stores over 50 gigabytes. But we're at 150 gigabytes today and expect to grow to a terabyte within the next two years. We've proved that SQL Server is an industry-strength platform that can scale."

With the ability to make faster, more accurate decisions about specific titles, HarperCollins has cut its return rate by half—from 30 percent to roughly 15 percent. Every percentage point means millions of dollars saved. The Microsoft-based knowledge-management solution has reduced development costs by 70 percent and has slashed more than $700,000 out of HarperCollins' annual IT budget. Using the Internet Information Server technology (in Microsoft Windows NT Server) and the Microsoft Visual InterDev Web development system, it takes HarperCollins days rather than months to develop and deploy applications. A serendipitous benefit was the elimination of tons of paper. Whereas all data before was delivered in thick paper reports, now it's delivered to users over the Web.

HarperCollins' positive experience with its data warehouse is enabling it to connect other areas of the company. "We're getting people off islands and helping them talk to one another," Anderson says. "Production data, sales data, inventory data: it's all available to everyone, so we can see trends, make intelligent decisions, and react a lot faster without the pain and angst we had before. This technology is really gluing the company together as never before."

DEMOGRAPHICS

Foster Parents Plan of Canada (FPP), a leading international fund-raiser for child-focused organizations, wanted to find a more efficient way to target prospective donors and serve them more effectively. A member of PLAN International, FPP gives Canadians the opportunity to sponsor a child and fund a variety of programs in developing countries. Designed to make a lasting difference in the lives of children, their families, and their communities, FPP programs support health care, education, access to clean water, housing, and micro credit. More than 90,000 Canadians sponsor 100,000 of the more than 1.1 million children worldwide who are helped by this international organization.

Although FPP has been around for more than 60 years and boasts an established donor base, competition for funding remains a challenge. At this writing, there are more than 70,000 registered charities in Canada, and that number is always rising. Moreover, what worked 20 years ago in reaching prospective donors does not necessarily work today. Communication tools are evolving, demographics are constantly shifting, and constituents are demanding faster communications and better customer service. FPP turned to its information technology (IT) department for help in getting fast access to information that could help the organization better respond to donor demands.

FOSTER PARENTS PLAN SNAPSHOT

Foster Parents Plan of Canada was forced to implement a knowledge-management solution in order to operate more effectively. It needed to uncover data buried in its systems in order to make better business decisions, such as how many children needed sponsors and so on. The company's data-warehouse solution gives employees real-time operational data and allows them to make well informed, timely decisions that decrease costs and improve efficiency. The following Microsoft products were used in the company's solution:

Operating Systems	■ Microsoft Windows 95
	■ Microsoft Windows NT Workstation
	■ Microsoft Windows NT Server
Productivity Applications	■ Microsoft Project
	■ Microsoft Internet Explorer
	■ Microsoft Office 95 and 97
Server Products	■ Microsoft SQL Server
	■ Microsoft SNA Server
	■ Microsoft Exchange Server

Digging Up Information

In the area of marketing strategies, FPP needed to first dig up valuable background information such as which communication vehicles work the best, how to retain sponsors, how many children currently require sponsors, and much more. To help accomplish these goals, the organization built a data warehouse to help turn raw operational data into meaningful, actionable business knowledge—knowledge that helps employees make fast, informed decisions and maximize organizational dollars. The FPP solution is built on a Microsoft SQL Server 7 database and other Microsoft BackOffice products, using Cognos business intelligence tools for desktop analysis.

With a legacy IT system housing its most critical data, FPP sought to set up an entirely new technology base. The organization knew it required a comprehensive knowledge-management strategy to put information at managers' fingertips. The system needed to be structured in a manner that would allow employees to spot trends and extract information needed for making decisions.

However, the information required for making decisions was located within the organization's AS/400 host applications. Kelvin Cantafio, chief information officer for Foster Parents Plan, explains, "While our AS/400 is great at taking in our operational data, it is often inefficient at outputting the available data for analysis purposes. Our departments need specific information on a daily, weekly, monthly, and ad hoc basis, which is difficult to extract from this host system." To stay efficient, the company's information had to be streamlined and better organized, to capture the natural flow of data and help deliver it to individuals with on-demand fluidity.

To get on top of a solution, Cantafio's staff worked in concert with Microsoft Certified Solution Provider M.R.S. Company Limited of Mississauga, Ontario. Together, they developed a data warehouse based on the Microsoft BackOffice family of products. Foster Parents Plan had standardized on Microsoft Office products back in 1996 to improve overall office productivity, so selecting BackOffice as its enterprise operating platform made sense and promised consistency for broader sharing of information internally. Several qualities needed to be threaded into the system to provide access to organizational data that can be easily dissected by all key business measures. A set of tools to effectively analyze and present information was also required. The organization knew that implementing these critical components would enable it to reach new heights.

Providing Systemic Access

Foster Parents Plan made sure that business people from all areas of the organization were represented on the data-warehouse team. "We needed to give key decision makers quick and easy access to critical information that allows them to make the most of our resources," Cantafio explains. "To make fast, accurate decisions that get results for our constituents and chew up a minimum of cycles, our managers need detailed breakdowns of important information about expenses, supporters, and resources. A data warehouse is a perfect vehicle for this."

M.R.S. helped implement the BackOffice portion of the solution. The provider's director of marketing and sales, Peter Christopoulos, says the solution has revamped Foster Parents Plan's IT structure and delivered an effective knowledge-management strategy. "This deployment has realized phenomenal results," he says. "Six months after we launched the pilot project, everyone was generating reports and analyzing information straight from the system. It has really improved the way FPP operates." Cantafio noted that under the new system, users themselves can get answers that used to require IT intervention. "We now call it self-serve information; it's empowering users to build their own reports, answer their own questions, without waiting on IT," he says. At FPP, the knowledge-management solution partnered technology with corporate cultures and business processes, so each aspect of the solution became a vehicle to manage and deliver the business information. The diversity of knowledge sources can now be embraced, giving it greater meaning through its relation to other information within the organization.

Cantafio has indicated that the FPP data marts have raised the bar of knowledge within the organization. "It's one thing to put Microsoft Windows in an organization. It's quite another to make operational data available to every business manager for analysis. By using real-time data to make real-time business decisions, we operate more efficiently and maximize the dollars we spend on programs."

WRAP UP

Knowledge-management systems make better decision making possible through analysis and collaboration:

■ By centralizing information, knowledge management connects the islands of data, simplifying access and making for more informed decisions.

■ An effective knowledge-management system helps knowledge workers analyze data at a more granular level than was previously possible.

■ Knowledge management puts the decision-making process where it belongs by making the data that knowledge workers require available to them.

■ Two key attributes of a knowledge-management system that supports business analysis are the timeliness and accuracy of the information it provides.

■ Simplicity improves turn-around time and therefore ensures that knowledge workers are more willing or even able to use the analysis tools available to them.

Taking Stock

1. Can your company define the competitive pressures on it?

2. Does your company have the ability to accurately forecast sales?

3. Is the information that your IT systems provide granular enough for knowledge workers to make good decisions?

4. Do your IT systems turn around reports in a timely manner so that decisions are also timely and knowledge workers don't hesitate to rely on them?

5. Is the data in your company centralized or is it contained in many islands?

ACTION PLAN

❑   Look at your company's data and determine whether it's connected. If it isn't, call your IT department to action to combine the data islands.

❑   Determine whether the people who *should* make decisions are equipped with the information they require for actually making those decisions.

❑   If your IT systems take hours or even days to compile reports, examine whether the combinations of products you learned about in this chapter can improve the turn-around time of those reports.

❑   Identify the groups of users who have or should have decision-making authority and determine the types of reports they need to make those decisions. Make sure those reports are available.

❑   If your IT systems require administrators to generate reports on behalf of users, ask your IT department to push responsibility for those reports to users.

Part III

Technology

Chapter 7

Digital Dashboard

Your car's dashboard, with its gauges, indicators, and blinking lights never more than a glance away, helps you make better, faster decisions as you're barreling down the freeway. Likewise, digital dashboards provide key information to knowledge workers so they can make better decisions quicker in fast-paced business climates.

Digital dashboards consolidate personal, team, corporate, and external information with single-click access to analytical and collaborative tools. Digital dashboards integrate views of companies' knowledge sources onto individuals' desktops, enabling them to make better decisions by providing immediate access to key information. In Microsoft's world, digital dashboards are customized solutions based on Microsoft Office (especially on Microsoft Outlook 2000). Microsoft Certified Solution Providers or in-house development staffs can tailor digital-dashboard solutions to the specific needs of any company, integrating its existing systems with the analytical and collaborative tools in products such as Office, Microsoft Exchange Server, and Microsoft SQL Server.

Digital dashboards are the first of Microsoft's four knowledge-management initiatives. The other three initiatives, which you will read about in this part of this book, are Exchange Web Storage System, wireless solutions, and intelligent interfaces.

With so much information from so many sources, knowledge workers can spend hours sifting through it just to find one key point. Digital dashboards prevent information overload by delivering focused, vital business information through the use of filters, user-specified categories, and summaries. Employees can access vital, high-level information through relevant business reports on a digital dashboard. And unlike browser-only portal solutions that deliver information from the Web or an intranet, digital dashboards integrate information from varieties of sources. Digital dashboards organize and make it easy to view key information from corporate applications, Web sites, team folders, and personal files. Digital dashboards also enable knowledge workers to leverage each other's knowledge. Organization-wide collaboration is more difficult for global corporations than for geographically centralized companies. Whether located in the office next door or on another continent, workers can use a digital dashboard to locate and communicate with experts, collaborate on projects, or research corporate presentations and documents. Because digital dashboards are based on Office, knowledge workers also have access to real-time tools such as Microsoft NetMeeting conferencing software and Microsoft Windows Media Services for communicating with coworkers and receiving training. Last, digital dashboards enable knowledge workers to make effective decisions where many of them get their most quality time: traveling. Digital dashboards give decision makers offline access to any source of information.

"We're all drowning in information. The challenge is to turn that information into knowledge and to empower our knowledge workers," says Daryl Ann Borel, assistant superintendent, Technology and Information Systems for the Houston Independent School District. HISD is now implementing a digital dashboard on a pilot basis. According to Borel, digital dashboards will help HISD meet that information challenge, making them extremely attractive to the school district.

As the benefits of digital dashboards surface through the easy availability of more precise information, they also become catalysts for a better understanding of information systems. For example, it often becomes apparent that key metrics to the corporate culture are not delivered effectively to employees in an accurate and timely manner, which can result in a lack of focus. Digital dashboards thus become a method through which information technology (IT) professionals can have a deeper, broader, and more measurable impact on the company. Here's an example in which digital dashboards have profound effects on workers' priorities. If a digital dashboard gives constant feedback about customer satisfaction, workers will become significantly more sensitive to this issue. Digital dashboards become a tool through which management can direct the focus of a corporation.

MICROSOFT OFFICE

Because digital dashboards are based on Office, they integrate the already familiar office-productivity suite with the Web. In their simplest forms, digital dashboards are dynamic Web pages in Outlook. They serve as windows to critical business information and leverage the rich analysis tools, collaboration capabilities, and Internet- and messaging-standards support built into Office. Office Web Components (OWCs) enable companies to publish spreadsheets, charts, and databases to the Web, where others can use a browser not only to view the documents but also to modify them and to manage data.

Outlook is Microsoft's popular mail and collaboration client. It enables users to store wide varieties of data—e-mail, appointments, contacts, notes, and so on—in folders. And because users can display any Web page in any folder to which they have access, Outlook is the perfect tool for building digital dashboards. The client's easy-to-use object model enables developers to create digital dashboards quickly, too. In short, Outlook is the dynamic portal through which knowledge workers view digital dashboards. The dashboard integrates data from different sources, including a stock ticker, a list of messages, and a sales chart. Imagine the possibilities of displaying in once place all the information that's most important to you each day, the information that affects your key business decisions.

HISD did imagine just that and more. They developed a digital dashboard for its administrators, superintendents, and principals to make key information available on their desktops. Their digital dashboard includes data that shows the average daily attendance per campus. It shows student performance on both state and national tests. It also provides information about lunch participation, e-mail, scheduling, and weather. HISD's digital dashboard will also be customizable to support the differing needs of different administrators. For example, administrators with an interest in grants and other financial sources might see them on their dashboards, with links to funding data on Web pages elsewhere and e-mail notification when grant information becomes available. Similarly, instructional administrators will be able to see Web sites with lesson-plan information and to receive e-mail notification when those sites are updated.

Outlook is just part of the story; Office also makes creating dashboard content simple for people with no development skills. Although creating basic Web pages is fairly easy for anyone, publishing *live* documents—interactive spreadsheets, charts, and databases—to the Web once required significant technical skill. OWCs enable users of all skill levels to publish interactive spreadsheets and databases directly to the Web. With OWCs, users can publish spreadsheets rather than routing them as e-mail attachments; publishing spreadsheets makes it possible for other workers in the organization to sort, filter, enter values for formula calculations, expand and collapse details, pivot, and so on—all from within Microsoft Internet Explorer.

PERSONAL DIGITAL DASHBOARDS

The latest trend is for independent software vendors (ISVs) to develop and market personal digital dashboards. These digital dashboards, as opposed to those created for workgroups or entire enterprises, are for individuals and rely solely on e-mail as a means to collaborate with other users. They provide the capability to search and organize e-mail. They also provide the ability to display information from various sources in a folder—typically Outlook Today.

One such example is the Personal Knowledge Portal from 80-20 Software (*http://www.80-20.com*). It helps you immediately begin using a digital dashboard to overcome e-mail chaos without disturbing the organization. In other words, it works within Outlook 2000 to organize and search through the plethora of information in your personal folders, but it does not require support on the server. Another example is MSNBC, which publishes a customizable digital dashboard. Using MSNBC's digital dashboard, you can view the latest news, sports, weather, and stock information in Outlook 2000—without looking for it on the Web. You can learn more about MSNBC's digital dashboard at *http://www.msnbc.com*.

Office Web Components

Increasingly, knowledge workers are turning to intranets and the Internet to share information with each another and with customers. In the Internet's early days, only technical staff understood how to create and publish Web pages. Knowledge workers were limited to using what they published. Change is coming, though, as products like Microsoft FrontPage make it possible for anyone to create and share documents on the Web. Office 2000 takes things a step forward. Microsoft Word, Microsoft Excel, Microsoft Access, and Microsoft PowerPoint support HTML as a native file format. And because Web server support is fully integrated into the Office File Save and File Open dialog boxes, publishing Office documents to Web servers is as easy as saving a file on your own computer's hard disk.

But publishing a spreadsheet or database document to the Web is only half the battle. The other half is enabling other people to interact with published documents and gain insight that's specific to them—not just to the publisher. For example, if you create a spreadsheet to analyze a product's profitability given various costs, an important aspect of sharing that spreadsheet is enabling other users to enter different values and recalculate the results. Likewise, if you create a PivotTable form, report, or query, an essential part of sharing these documents is enabling other users to sort, filter, pivot, or enter their own values.

Alone, Web browsers can't sort, filter, or recalculate totals on Web pages; but with OWCs, they can. OWCs, illustrated in Figure 7-1 on the next page, are a collection of COM (Component Object Model) objects that enable the publishing of spreadsheets, charts, and databases to the Web. They take full advantage of the rich interactivity provided by Internet Explorer. When you use Internet Explorer to browse a Web page that contains an OWC, you interact with the page right in your browser; you can sort, filter, enter values for formula calculations, expand and collapse details, pivot, and so on. The COM controls provide the interactivity. Each OWC is fully programmable, enabling Office Solution Providers to build rich, interactive, Web-based solutions. OWCs include a spreadsheet, a PivotTable dynamic view, a data source, and a chart:

- **Spreadsheet** The spreadsheet component provides a recalculation engine, a full-function library, and a simple spreadsheet user interface in Web pages. Calculations can refer to spreadsheet cells or to any control on the page or URL via the Internet Explorer document object model. Office users create Web pages with spreadsheet components by saving Excel workbooks as Web pages and by selecting the option to publish the page interactively.

- **PivotTable** The PivotTable dynamic-views component enables users to analyze information by sorting, grouping, filtering, outlining, and pivoting. The data can come from a spreadsheet range, from a relational database (an Access or Microsoft SQL Server database), or from any data source that supports multidimensional OLE DB (such as Microsoft Decision Support Server). When an Excel user saves a PivotTable or QueryTable dynamic view as an interactive Web page, the page contains a PivotTable component. Web pages with PivotTable components can also be created in the designer for Data Access Pages in Access.

- **Data Source** The data-source component is the reporting engine behind Data Access Pages and the PivotTable component. It manages communication with back-end database servers and determines which database records can be displayed on the page. For example, if a Data Access Page displays orders by customer, the data source component retrieves the order records for the customer being displayed and manages the sorting, filtering, and updating of those records in response to user actions. The data-source component relies on Microsoft Active Data Objects (ADO) for "plumbing," and, like all the Office Web Components, it is fully programmable.

■ **Chart**   The chart component graphically displays information from the spreadsheet, from the PivotTable dynamic views, or from the data-source component. Because it is bound directly to other controls on the page, the chart component updates instantly in response to user interactions with the other components. For example, you can chart a PivotTable view that displays sales by region. Then, in the browser, you can pivot to display sales by product, and the chart will update automatically without round-tripping to the Web server. When an Excel user saves a workbook containing a chart as an interactive Web page, the page contains a chart component. Office Web Component charts can also be created and edited directly in the Data Access Pages designer.

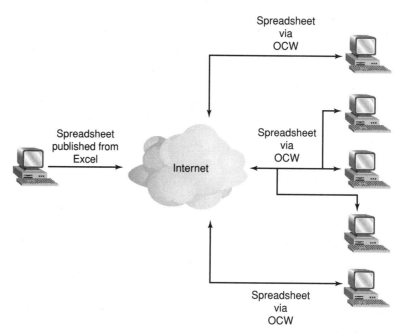

Figure 7-1. *Office Web Components.*

Outlook Team Folders

Workers can collaborate using Outlook in ways other than publishing documents on the Web. Outlook Team Folders enables users to organize and share information with other knowledge workers. Some of the features include the following:

- **Collaboration** Teams have one place to go to set up meetings, access documents, check on tasks, and access project-related contacts lists.

- **Calendaring** With the calendaring feature, you can post team members' schedules to the team folder. When setting up meetings, you can instantly see who is available when. This feature helps you schedule appointments simply and easily, without spending precious hours tracking down a mutually convenient time.

- **Document Sharing** Now all relevant information and documentation can be placed in one location, accessible by those with permission. Web pages, spreadsheets, word-processing documents, and other formatted material are available around the clock by those who need it.

- **Discussions** Wherever you are, you can have real-time, online discussions with members of your team. Instead of relying on the exchange of e-mail, threaded discussions allow instant communication.

- **Tasks** Let team members know their roles, tasks, and schedule. With a team task list, team members have instant access to their contribution to the project.

- **Contact Management** Have one place for team members to access the list of contacts important to the project. As the project moves forward, you can easily update the list so everyone on the team has the names and contact information of the people involved.

Outlook Team Folders combines the data-storage capabilities of Exchange Server with an intuitive, Web-based functionality. To achieve this mix of storage function and Web interface, team folders actually reside in two locations: on the computer running Exchange Server—for data access and storage; and on a Web server—for a Web page interface.

Outlook Team Folders starts with a team folder's home page, which is actually a Web page viewed within Outlook. Similar to the Outlook Today feature, this page enables users to view information in other folders, along with other Web pages, using the Outlook interface. It also means that, at a glance, users get a summary of the activity in different folders. With the Outlook View Control, which is a component of Outlook Team Folders, the Web-based team-folder home page can host Exchange Server data and other Web-based data, taking advantage of the richness of Outlook views. From the team folder's home page, users can access all information in the team folders by simply clicking links.

MICROSOFT BACKOFFICE SERVER

Outlook is the most visible part of a digital dashboard, but Microsoft BackOffice works behind the scenes to make it all happen. BackOffice is a family of best-of-breed server products, optimized for Microsoft Windows 2000 Server, that provide the server foundation for a company's knowledge-management solutions. The BackOffice family provides three benefits. First, BackOffice offers a broad range of capabilities, including e-mail and collaboration; databases; Internet access; desktop management; Web search and content management; and host connectivity. Second, BackOffice products are fully integrated with Windows 2000 Server, meaning that there is only one set of user accounts to manage, a consistent security model spans family members, and administrators can use familiar Windows 2000 Server tools for application-server management. BackOffice also integrates well with an existing UNIX, AS/400, or mainframe environment, and it provides access to existing databases and applications. Last, the BackOffice family of products take advantage of the Windows operating system to reduce administrative complexity. BackOffice also integrates well with Office, making it easy for end users to be productive when managing e-mail, analyzing databases, and creating Web content.

Appendix A, "Microsoft Platform," provides more technical information about how each part of BackOffice fulfills the requirements of a knowledge-management solution. This appendix looks at BackOffice from the perspective of a company building a knowledge-management solution and shopping for technology. Figure 7-2 is a diagram you'll see again in Appendix A. It shows how the knowledge desktop, knowledge services, and the system fit together to enable knowledge management. With regard to digital dashboards, Outlook is the knowledge desktop. The components of BackOffice are responsible for implementing the knowledge services and the system in this diagram. They provide centralized management of companies' core knowledge assets and enable seamless delivery and tracking of those assets. Here's how those services relate to each component in BackOffice:

■ **Collaboration** Office and Microsoft Exchange are integrated with collaborative capabilities that enable users to innovate together within their familiar desktop tools. These products provide capabilities such as shared calendars and task lists, threaded discussions, easy application creation, and folder home pages to help groups collaborate. In addition, Microsoft NetMeeting contains tools for white boarding, video, chat, and application sharing, all of which enable users to communicate and work together on knowledge assets as they collaborate.

■ **Content Management** Content-management technologies enable people to capture, codify, and organize experiences and ideas in central repositories that enable seamless, intuitive access to an entire organization. Exchange, Microsoft Site Server, and Office integrate to provide the ability to categorize, publish, and manage documents and content. Microsoft's knowledge-management platform also supports workflow around content, such as versioning, approvals, routing, and locking.

■ **Analysis** Quickly spotting trends in financial and line-of-business data enables decision makers to plan better strategies. The data warehousing and business-intelligence features in Office and SQL enable knowledge workers at all levels of a corporation to better understand their markets. Data Transformation Services enables SQL users to analyze data from any ODBC-compliant system. Microsoft OLAP (Online Analytical Processing), Microsoft PivotTable Services, and Office Web Components enable users to analyze vast amounts of data in their familiar Office or browser environments.

■ **Search and Deliver** Building teams and communities across a dispersed organization is possible with portals built on personalized, cross-enterprise search and delivery technologies. Site Server searches across databases, public folders, Web sites, and file shares. In addition, it also can deliver personalized information to either community portals or directly to users' desktops.

■ **Tracking and Workflow** Tracking services enable companies to identify best practices by measuring successes, while workflow tools enable the creation of process-based applications to ensure that the practices are followed and measured. Exchange Folder Agents and Routing Objects combine to provide a powerful and flexible system for building workflow applications.

BackOffice and Office provide all the technologies necessary for building a knowledge-management solution, and they are at the heart of Microsoft's knowledge-management platform. Also, the Team Productivity Update combines with Office and BackOffice Server to produce collaborative, centralized, and secure team workspaces for line-of-business data, tracking applications, documents, issues, and online discussions. The Team Productivity Update extends the new collaboration features within Office, enabling teams to get faster results through a central location for sharing team information.

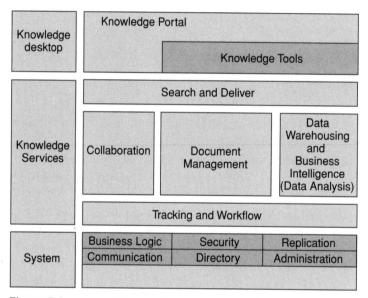

Figure 7-2. *A typical knowledge-management platform.*

Collaboration

Knowledge workers must be able to send e-mail reliably, securely, and quickly. The system must support fast responses, rules, multiple formats and styles (rich text, HTML, and so on). It must also provide the ability to sign and encrypt messages, and it must be able to organize the flood of information arriving by e-mail. Thus, requirements include reliability, high performance, security, scalability, and interoperability with—and migration from—existing messaging systems.

Organizations also look for a growing spectrum of collaborative capabilities that are not necessarily tied to messaging.

- **Individual productivity** Calendars, contact lists, and one-to-one information sharing.

- **Team productivity** Group scheduling, shared task lists, and shared contact lists.

- **Departmental productivity** Discussion groups and real-time collaboration.

- **Enterprise productivity** Routing, workflow, and document management.

Companies can extend these features to Web-based scenarios that include structured data and transacted applications by using Collaboration Data Objects (CDO), Active Data Objects (ADO), and Microsoft Transaction Server (MTS) with Microsoft Message Queue Server (MSMQ)—technologies within Windows NT Server. For instance, a collaboration solution for project management enables a company to react to changing business conditions. It makes users more productive with near-instant access to information. It manages information by providing structure to data, enables users to collaborate in real time (no matter where they are in the world), and enables them to make better-informed decisions.

Content Management

Getting users and customers connected to corporate data and enabling them to interact with it effectively is a driving goal of knowledge management. Using Web-based applications as well as publishing and management methods, administrators can bring together new and legacy systems to provide users with access to databases, corporate directories, documents, discussions, process applications (forms), and more. With these tools, users can create, publish, search, and manage information easily. Administrators and publishers can deliver, manage, and analyze the Web site and data.

Word, Windows 2000 Server's Internet Information Services, Index Server, Site Server, and the Microsoft Office Server Extensions are the key enabling technologies for building an information-publishing solution that provides simple and seamless data access and interactivity to users. The same technologies could also help establish or polish a corporate presence on the Internet, such as an investor-information site, where content is provided externally to customers and updated on a regular basis by a variety of people within the organization.

Business Intelligence

All organizations need to have access to timely and reliable data to make decisions. Data-center managers think about collecting relevant data, storing it, staging it for future use, and making it available for users to extract, manipulate, and analyze. Business users and administrators look at exploiting this information via analysis tools, data marts, and data warehouses. Developers build workflow-type applications (such as document routing) or information-management systems such as Decision Support Systems (DSS).

Knowledge workers must be able to obtain data easily for analysis using familiar tools. They shouldn't have to rely on the IT department to create complex front ends to corporate databases. By using Office applications, employees have full access to data and the tools to analyze industry-wide, corporate, and even departmental data. In addition, employees should be able to communicate and collaborate on data analysis, in real time, with other employees—either from headquarters or remotely. For example, a decision-support system for sales analysis could allow anyone to examine sales data and make better decisions based on that data.

Together, Office and BackOffice provide rich data-analysis capabilities. Office supports connecting to back-end databases by using component-based middleware. OLE DB and ADO provide better performance against SQL Server and other OLE DB providers, so developers can easily create powerful applications. Office also takes a client/server approach to dealing with very large databases, retrieving only the data the user wants to see instead of the entire data set. And support for OLAP in Office 2000 enables it to work tightly with SQL Server-based data marts and data warehouses. Users can display a PivotTable dynamic view in Microsoft Excel for high-performance data analysis. This enables them to make complicated queries against large amounts of data and across many dimensions (time and geography, for example) and to get answers quickly. Microsoft OLAP server technology, which is part of SQL Server, provides OLAP services.

Tracking and Workflow

As the Web becomes more pervasive in everyday productivity, knowledge workers recognize intranet technology as a unique and fast way to gather, track, and share information quickly. Organizations require workflow-type applications (such as document routing) or an information-management system such as sales-force automation tools (lead-tracking systems and expense reporting) to support data tracking. Historically, accessing data from an enterprise-level database was challenging for anyone other than a database administrator or IT professional. Using Office as the front-end for data access and corporate reporting systems makes it possible to get more directly involved.

For example, sales-force automation or sales-tracking tools enable a company's sales force to develop relationships with customers and delivers access to the most up-to-date information possible. They help the company remain competitive in a fast-paced marketplace by helping it remain in touch with its customers and supplies and by allowing knowledge workers to make better decisions faster. Combined, Office and BackOffice provide features that simplify the creation of powerful tracking applications:

- Access supports OLE DB, enabling users to combine the ease of use of the Access interface with the scalability of back-end enterprise databases, such as Microsoft SQL Server, without needing to go through the Jet database.

- The Access user interface lets workers create a new type of file (.adp) that connects directly to the integrated store available in Office or SQL Server. This makes creating true client/server applications easier.

- Microsoft updated many popular Access wizards to support new client/server tasks, such as creating a new database, report, or form. When users work in a Microsoft Access project, they use new design tools to create and manage server-side objects, including tables, views, stored procedures, and database diagrams.

- Application developers can build custom workflow solutions to automate business tasks, create more effective teams, and make better use of the knowledge available throughout an enterprise. Exchange Server and Outlook provide a comprehensive set of tools for building workflow applications, including the Exchange Scripting Agent and Routing Objects, and the Outlook drag-and-drop tools, with full support for Visual Basic Scripting for creating electronic forms.

- Data Access Pages are interactive, dynamically linked HTML pages that let users analyze and manipulate data from within a Web browser. Data can be included within the context of the page or linked from a SQL Server database. Developers can store pages on a Web server or file system, in Exchange Public Folders, or as e-mail attachments.

DASHBOARD DEVELOPMENT

To get the ball rolling, take a look at the samples in Microsoft's Digital Dashboard Starter Kit. This kit comes with the documentation, files, and samples necessary to hit the ground running. Free of charge, the kit is available for download from *http://www.microsoft.com/business*. Using this kit or viewing its samples requires no technical skills. The samples do require Outlook 2000, however. If you're not comfortable evaluating the kit yourself, pass it on to someone in the IT department and have them evaluate it. Let them wow you with the types of information they can put on your desktop. This is precisely where Oregon State University started its work.

Oregon State University is an example of an organization that's leading the digital-dashboard revolution. The school wants to use technology to give students, faculty, and administrators competitive advantages by helping them master the plethora of information they must assimilate. The school is doing so successfully because it's adopting the digital dashboard as part of its knowledge-management solution. Greg Scott, the information services manager for the school, says that they wanted to make the network easier for everyone to access; they adopted the digital dashboard because it helps the school provide a single point through which to access files and information.

Scott consulted students, MIS department faculty, and a key administrator to help refine ideas for the two digital-dashboard versions they were contemplating: one for students, which provides class information and collaborative communications with faculty and other students, and one for staff, which helps manage projects that involve coordination of documents, tasks, and calendars. Scott had numerous people examining prototypes, and their feedback validated the developers' work. According to Scott, "One management professor reminded us that *less is more*. That was very helpful because there's a tendency to treat this like a Christmas tree and hang ornaments all over the place, inundating people with data. We're focusing on only key metrics to keep a streamlined design."

For more information about managing and developing knowledge-management solutions, and overcoming cultural barriers to this kind of innovation, see Chapter 2, "Organizational Barriers." This chapter shows how to manage expectations, develop a prototype, and get the whole organization behind your effort.

PRODUCTS FOR DASHBOARDS

Microsoft Office 2000 provides the user interface for a digital dashboard. Outlook 2000 is the typical messaging and collaboration client, while users can use Office Web Components to publish dynamic documents to an intranet. The combination of Office 2000 and each of the following Microsoft products is available for building digital dashboards and are in fact typical components:

- **Microsoft Exchange Server** Provides the backend for Outlook 2000 and allows users to create shared team folders for documents, discussions, project tasks, and so on. The integration between Outlook and Exchange Server enables users to take folders offline when they travel and synchronize when they return.

- **Microsoft SQL Server** Enables knowledge workers to connect directly to business data and analyze it as required. OLAP provides sophisticated and flexible analysis using familiar tools such as Microsoft Excel.

Developing the Prototype

Developing the prototype dashboard was very easy, according to Scott, because his team is working with familiar Microsoft tools—such as the Microsoft Visual InterDev Web development system—and because of the technology updates that Microsoft offers as part of the digital-dashboard initiative, including the Digital Dashboard Starter Kit, Team Folder Wizard, and Team Productivity Update for the BackOffice family. They leveraged the samples and wizards that Microsoft provides, speeding up development. Scott says that it would have taken two months to do what they did in a single week. Part of their success, and the short amount of time in which they realized it, is due to the ability to borrow code directly from the digital-dashboard samples in the Digital Dashboard Starter Kit. The Team Folder Wizard also saved them weeks of development work. Scott adds, "We found the examples especially helpful in giving us ideas and as a construction resource."

To create their prototype, Scott's team is using one of the starter-kit samples as a base, cutting and pasting existing controls, object tags, and parameters, and changing the labels as appropriate to reflect their specific needs. They're using the Team Folders Wizard to create the customized folders that hold information, such as reading lists, and interactive components, such as instructor/student and student/student e-mail discussion threads. The wizard walks instructors through the process of creating team folders for each class, virtually generating each folder and then allowing them to name it and to specify its location.

Scott says he regards team folders as an advance over the Exchange Public Folders that the school used to disseminate course-related material and as a collection point for students to submit their work. Team folders permit far more collaboration and dynamically update themselves to reflect modifications created on-the-fly by instructors. Faculty can easily set permissions, links, and other parameters. Folders can even integrate with Microsoft NetMeeting conferencing software for enhanced interactivity in online discussions. Instructors had the option to create and use online discussions before this, but without the simple and fully integrated interface of the digital dashboard, they were less likely to do so. Public folders required students and faculty to drill down through the folders' view, sort through all the class public folders, and find the right material.

With the digital dashboard and team folders, this isn't necessary. Students and faculty look under their class *nugget*—the dashboard's basic unit of organization, which can be any dynamic data, such as Microsoft ActiveX technologies, ASP, or XML—to see all the course information necessary for that class. The faculty will use team folders more frequently because the school enabled discussions within those folders. The ease of creating team folders also led Scott's team to experiment with them more broadly. They can house team folders on separate Active Server Pages (server-side scripts in Internet Information Server) or combine them into a single set, based on how much information the designers want to provide to users at once. Being able to quickly compose prototype folders enabled Scott's team to create various designs and share them with potential users for feedback, enabling better, user-friendly results.

Creating the Dashboard

Norman Rankis is the CIO of Centenary College. He met with members of Microsoft's Higher Education staff to review the school's existing information reports and to adapt and elaborate on that content to develop *health indicators* that are meaningful to Centenary. For financial aid, for example, that meant expanding the available information to show how well financial-aid distribution at any time matched the school's strategic plan for its student population. Rankis then brought in Microsoft Consulting Services (MCS) to look at the college's infrastructure and to recommend hardware to support the dashboard. On the recommendation of MCS, the college installed a Compaq server to support this first dashboard project. "The MCS plan was like a plug that fit right into our environment," says Rankis.

According to Rankis, development was straightforward, due in part to the Digital Dashboard Starter Kit. Rankis used his existing databases for enrollment, financial aid, and retention, and he developed simple SQL programs to query his third-party, commercial databases. The digital dashboard integrates the data from queries and populates the dashboard components.

Institutional-aid data comes from one of those third-party packages, the College Boards PowerFaids Financial Aid System. An industry standard that's updated regularly to reflect new federal regulations for financial aid, the software was part of the university's IT infrastructure and works flawlessly with the digital dashboard. The software reports both budgeted and actual breakdowns for both categories within Institutional Aid: new and returning students. "The nice thing about the digital dashboard is that it shows key data at a glance, and if the executive needs to pull down the entire Institutional Aid budget, he can, right from the dashboard," says Rankis. The dashboard's data on enrollment, retention, and receivables all come from CAMS (Comprehensive Academic Management System), a Three Rivers Systems Inc. package widely used by small colleges and universities. "The dashboard design doesn't care from which sub-system the data is coming," notes Rankis. "As long as we can populate the spreadsheet data, the dashboard works."

Rankis chose this particular initial approach—isolating the digital dashboard from third-party software—to ensure that the school was not infringing on copyright or contractual use of that software by exposing its database structures, especially if the school later makes its design available to other institutions. Although the intermediate data-import layer was a concession to this practical issue, Rankis says it resulted in the cleanest, most robust structure for the information system. The program runs automatically on a regular update cycle far in excess of the frequency provided by paperbound alternatives.

WRAP UP

■ The term *digital dashboard* is much newer than the ability to combine data sources within a specific user interface. Decision support systems are not new. What make digital dashboards so exciting are the possibilities that combining different aspects of knowledge management provide.

■ Digital dashboards consolidate personal, team, business, and other types of information, and they provide a single user interface from which to access it all.

■ Knowledge workers are more likely to focus on the business's priorities if the information required to make decisions in support of those priorities is readily available.

■ Digital dashboards can display data from numerous, unrelated sources in one user interface, helping knowledge workers gain more insight from what they see.

■ Digital dashboards are easy to build, and the Digital Dashboard Starter Kit provides plenty of samples from which you can build your own dashboard.

■ Office Web Components (OWCs) enable any user, regardless of skill, to publish interactive information that's suitable for a digital dashboard.

■ Outlook Team Folders help users organize and share information by providing for shared collaboration, calendaring, document sharing, discussions, shared task lists, and contact management.

■ Behind the scenes, BackOffice supports digital dashboards by providing knowledge services for collaboration, content management, analysis, searching, and workflow management.

Taking Stock

1. Do you have a highly visible group that can pilot a digital dashboard?

2. Does your business have someone to champion the use of digital dashboards?

3. Have you identified the most important knowledge sources for each group?

4. Will you require different digital dashboards for different groups?

5. Is your business replacing a knowledge portal or starting fresh?

6. Does your business use or plan to deploy the Office family of products?

7. Does your business have the infrastructure available to support digital dashboards?

8. Is a development staff available to create a digital dashboard for your business?

9. Have you conducted a needs assessment to confirm business requirements?

ACTION PLAN

❏ Download and experiment with the samples in the Digital Dashboard Starter Kit, and read *Digital Dashboard Business Process Assessment Guide*. Both resources are available at *http://www.microsoft.com/business*.

❏ Identify the different digital dashboards that your business will require. It's likely that you'll require different digital dashboards for different disciplines.

❏ Get key employees from each department involved in the design process.

❏ Identify the knowledge sources that must be available on each digital dashboard. For example, a digital dashboard for sales might include sales projections while a digital dashboard for development might include project-management statistics.

❏ Create a plan for your company's digital dashboards.

Chapter 8

Microsoft Exchange Web Storage System

Web Storage System unifies e-mail, documents, and other knowledge sources in a single repository that knowledge workers can access through any application that supports Internet-based standards.

Web Storage System, one of Microsoft's key knowledge-management initiatives, removes barriers to collaboration that knowledge workers face today. It combines the features of a file system, the Web, and a collaboration server into a single location for storing and managing information as well as building and running applications. This platform for managing information includes consistent mechanisms for searching, categorizing, and retrieving data. Web Storage System is a new feature in Microsoft Exchange Server, which includes other new features that help companies build knowledge-management solutions.

Specifically, Web Storage System provides a single repository for managing e-mail, documents, Web pages, and other resources within one infrastructure, integrating knowledge sources in a single location. It supports offline access, remote client access, and support for a range of APIs that enable developing knowledge-management solutions. Also, Web Storage System serves as a platform for unified messaging, which enables knowledge workers to access personal information, such as their calendar and contacts, as well as e-mail and voicemail messages. Knowledge-management solutions typically require three key services. First, they require file system services that enable the knowledge desktop to read and write documents as well as store streaming data such as audio, video, and so on. File system services include a data model that supports hierarchical and heterogeneous collections (folders containing any type of item in any folder). Knowledge-management solutions also require database services to provide queries beyond what is possible on files in the file system. Database services include atomic updates that enable applications to present a consistent view to knowledge workers when updates involve more than one item in Web Storage System. Last, knowledge-management solutions require collaboration services to provide messaging, contact, calendaring support, and real-time collaboration.

Web Storage System is the second of Microsoft's four knowledge-management initiatives. The other three initiatives, which you read about in this part of this book, are digital dashboards, wireless solutions, and intelligent interfaces.

Web Storage System provides all these services in one well-integrated package, making it easier for knowledge workers to find, use, and share information. Developers can use Web Storage System to expand their use of Microsoft Exchange, Microsoft Office, and Microsoft BackOffice as platforms for knowledge management and to provide a wide range of business solutions that lower the total cost of ownership and improve productivity throughout an enterprise. For more information about how Office and BackOffice fit into Microsoft's knowledge-management initiatives, see Chapter 7, "Digital Dashboards," which describes other platform components.

WEB STORAGE SYSTEM

Web Storage System adds numerous features to Exchange that enable companies to build knowledge-management solutions using Microsoft's knowledge-management platform. The sections that follow describe these new features and capabilities:

- Standards Support
- Rich HTML

- Win32 Interfaces

- Advanced Scripting

- Streaming Store

- Content Indexing

Standards Support

Web Storage System provides an important feature for any knowledge-management solution: the ability to access any item in Web Storage System via HTTP, the protocol that Web browsers use to download documents on the Internet. Support for HTTP means that any Web browser, including digital dashboards, can display documents in the Web Storage System. Also, every item in Web Storage System has a unique, readable address associated with it, making that item easy to retrieve.

With current Web servers, such as Microsoft Windows 2000 Server and Microsoft Internet Information Server, developers must enable HTTP requests to access files or records. But Web Storage System provides out-of-the-box integration with Web servers, enabling developers to make each item in Web Storage System accessible without having to write a single line of code. In addition, Web Storage System can be accessed through the DAV (Distributed Authoring and Versioning) extensions to HTTP found in Microsoft Internet Information Server 5. DAV makes development easier.

Web Storage System is also an XML store. Its support for XML provides content in an Internet-standard format. This makes providing data access services to developers who need to query and modify information in Web Storage System easier.

Rich HTML

Extending its support for Internet-based standards, Web Storage System automatically provides an HTML 3.2 view of a folder and its objects based on each item's properties. Also, Web Storage System provides native support for advanced Web browsers that support HTML 4. This support enables administrators to provide knowledge workers with Web-based access to its content. In this figure, you see a view of Web Storage System within Internet Explorer.

Win32 Interfaces

Web Storage System supports the same interfaces that developers use to read and write data to the file system. Doing so enables developers to leverage functionality that's already available in the file system. For example, in writing for Microsoft Windows, developers can use Win32 APIs such as *CreateFile*, *ReadFile*, and *WriteFile*.

The kicker is that administrators can share data in Web Storage System the same way they share files on a file server. They use the commands net share, net use, and so on. Alternatively, they can share Web Storage System files using the operating system's interface, which is easier to use but not scriptable. This enables developers to port Web applications that they built solely around the file system to Web Storage System simply by changing the virtual directory.

Last, support for Win32 programming interfaces is beneficial to knowledge workers. It enables them to use tools with which they're already familiar to access their documents, e-mail, messages, and other types of files.

Advanced Scripting

Most Web applications require more functionality than what's available through Win32's programming interfaces and support for the file system. For example, numerous Web applications use scripts to add complex behaviors rather than serving up static HTML documents. (Mouse rollovers, outlines, and other navigational features are examples.) By making every item in Web Storage System accessible by an address, Web Storage System supports ASP (Active Server Pages.) An example of an ASP script is one that returns a different Web page depending on the user's client and one that processes a form that a user submits. Scripting support involves more complexity than merely the ability to host ASPs, however.

In addition, Web Storage System supports the same database interfaces used by ADO scripts in building data-intensive Web applications. Web Storage System comes with an OLE DB 2.5 provider that supports ADO scripting, as well as database services such as SQL query support and transaction support. The Web Storage System query support includes full-text content indexing to enable efficient retrieval of all items that contain a string for a single folder or for a hierarchy of folders.

Streaming Store

No longer are e-mail messages just unformatted text. They include large attachments, multimedia, voice files, and even rich HTML formatting. These new capabilities enrich knowledge workers' messaging and collaboration experience, but they place a heavy burden on any system, regardless of how much iron you throw at it.

Web Storage System's streaming-store feature addresses this truth by enabling it to natively store very large messages and attachments. Client programs access multimedia data more quickly through file-streaming interfaces, increasing the performance and scalability of a system that uses Web Storage System. For example, Web Storage System enables the streaming-media feature of PowerPoint 2000, which enables users to save PowerPoint slides as NetShow files. The streaming store helps ensure the fidelity of data and lowers the number of file conversions.

Also, Web Storage System enables administrators to provide streaming-media support directly from Web Storage System. This means that administering and managing streaming resources are the same as managing any other type of Web Storage System content.

Content Indexing

Web Storage System provides fast searches and lookups by managing indexes for common key fields. Microsoft Outlook users can search for documents in the Web Storage System as easily as they can search for messages today. They can be more productive. With full-text search, Outlook text searches become extremely fast. For example, Outlook searches that once took several minutes now take seconds. Additionally, Outlook indexes and searches all the text in attachments.

ADMINISTRATION

Managing a single, unified storage system based on Web Storage System enables IT administrators to reduce total cost of ownership (TCO). Costs for backup, restore, and other routine maintenance will naturally decline as administrators need to manage only one storage engine for multiple applications. As shown in Figure 8-1, Web Storage System enables centralized administration. Training costs will drop and the maintenance learning curve will soften, as administrators no longer have to manage mail servers, file servers, and Web servers separately to host knowledge workers' data. Web Storage System gives companies a single repository for all this and more.

If you deploy Web Storage System as a unified storage engine, knowledge workers will be able to store e-mail messages, documents, Web pages, and collaborative information in the same shared storage. This process is invisible to users, even though they save data using different clients, such as Outlook, Internet Explorer, Microsoft Word, and so on. If all back-end servers are Web Storage System servers, administrators need to learn only one toolset to configure, monitor, back up, and restore one type of server. This reduces long-term training costs and lowers the learning curve for both new and experienced IT administrators.

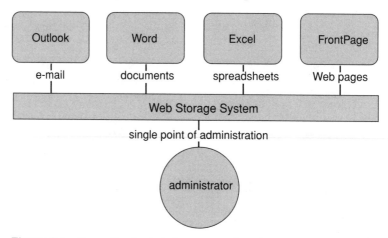

Figure 8-1. *Centralized administration with Web Storage System.*

Web Storage System extends all the management features traditionally available for messaging and collaboration data into document storage of all kinds. Administrators can easily configure things like data-replication topology, database-storage quotas, and granular administrative and access control.

As far as administration goes, your IT department will be more concerned with a few abstract concepts. The next sections will discuss some of those concepts in more detail:

- **Scalability** How performance grows with additional resources.
- **Reliability** How long the system runs without failing.
- **Security** How protected the system is from intrusion as well as accidents.
- **Integration** How well the system integrates with other systems.

Scalability

Web Storage System enables administrators to distribute storage across multiple physical databases, a design feature that provides numerous advantages. Web Storage System can grow in a virtual sense while limiting risk and maintaining granular control by using multiple databases to keep individual database sizes small. Multiple databases also decrease backup and recovery time, helping ensure conformity to service-level agreements while enabling your business to scale servers easily. Your server capacity is limited only by the amount of hardware storage available, as Figure 8-2 shows. Increasing the virtual-storage capacity of the Web Storage System by distributing data on multiple databases and servers is invisible to knowledge workers.

Multiple databases also provide administrators a wider range of design flexibility. Administrators have a plethora of ways to distribute data across multiple databases available to Web Storage System. Administrators can target databases at specific classes of users. For example, on a particular server, data for executives might be hosted on a set of databases different from those that hold data used by other employees. This enables administrators to control the configuration of each database, such as the content-indexing settings, data-retention intervals, and folder-storage limits. Also, they can control service levels and outage time due to failure by limiting the amount of data that users can store in each database.

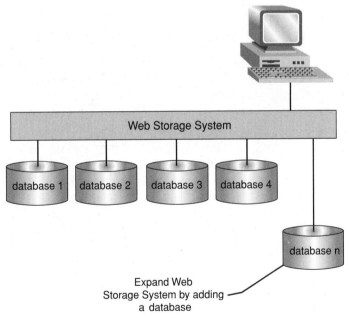

Figure 8-2. *Distributing Web Storage System databases.*

Alternatively, administrators can randomly distribute data across all databases in Web Storage System, minimizing the impact of a disaster to any one particular department or function of an organization. For instance, three storage databases can equally share data for the finance, accounting, and legal departments. If there is a failure in any one of these databases, none of the departments is critically impaired. In either example, administrators maintain control over which data resides in a particular database and determining the configuration parameters of each database.

Reliability

Web Storage System gives your business unprecedented reliability, even as it scales, and ensures the integrity of mission-critical data. Web Storage System supports transaction logging at the database level. It uses write-ahead transaction logs to ensure data integrity through redundancy and to provide transactional security. Committed transactions, such as saving an item in a folder, are written to disk with assurance. Temporary interruptions such as power failures won't cause data loss, because Web Storage System can replay the transaction logs to restore data into the database files.

Within folders, Web Storage System supports data replication so that even if one of your servers is down, replicas of that data exist on other servers. Additionally, replication management enables administrators to effectively load balance application access. Web Storage System also improves reliability through support for multiple databases, which you read about in the previous section. Using multiple databases means that a failure in a single database results in little impact to the overall down time of a larger system, removing the fabled single point of failure. Web Storage System can restore the failed database while the other databases remain mounted and in service. Figure 8-3 illustrates a scenario whereby Web Storage System replicates data across three databases, and if any of them fails, the system remains up and running.

At the system level, Web Storage System fully supports Windows 2000 clustering. Web Storage System on one server can accept control over the data being managed by Web Storage System on another server that has just experienced a failure, minimizing down time. And the processing of failing over to the other server is invisible to users.

Security

Web Storage System extends Windows 2000's security model to individual items and fields. Based on Windows 2000 Access Control Lists (ACLs), administrators can grant or deny permission for users to read, write, edit, or delete specific items. Administrators can determine users' views of a folder's contents on an item-by-item and even by a field-by-field basis.

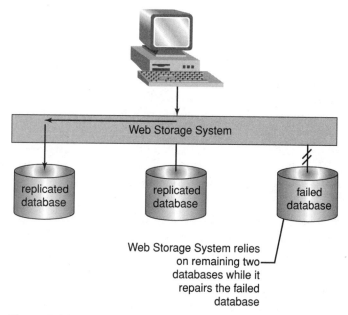

Figure 8-3. *Web Storage System Replication*

Note that Web Storage System uses native Windows 2000 ACLs. Administrators must manage only a single set of security groups, and those groups apply to data stored in both Web Storage System and Windows 2000 file shares. In fact, they can use the ACL editor in Windows Explorer to set permissions on individual items in Web Storage System. Once again, a single paradigm for security management enables customers to control and reduce administrative training costs.

Integration

Microsoft designed Web Storage System for optimal management within Windows 2000. It can fully leverage Active Directory configuration information while respecting the security settings enabled by Windows 2000 ACLs. Those who are already familiar with Windows 2000 administration will find supporting and managing Web Storage System simple, because many of the concepts are the same. As you've already read, Web Storage System is fully integrated with the Windows 2000 security infrastructure and the file-system infrastructure, and it supports management via Active Directory and Microsoft Management Console.

ACTIVE DIRECTORY

Active Directory is the directory service in Windows 2000 Server. Windows NT Server 4 and earlier versions didn't have a directory service. Active Directory enables easier and more centralized administration. For example, rather than using one program to administer users, another to administer computers, and yet another to manage policies, administrators do all of those things by using Active Directory Users and Computers. Active Directory catalogs everything on the network, so administrators can manage the network from a single point (even their own desktop), instead of managing each domain controller separately.

Users see Active Directory not as an administrative tool but as a catalog of everything that's on the network. It includes printers, other users, computers, and so on. Users can search the directory to find the printer nearest them with certain features, for example, or they can more easily find the computer that contains particular files.

Active Directory makes networks simpler and more secure. It provides the infrastructure for a network's security, including technologies such as Kerberos, a protocol that authenticates users when they log on to the network. It also allows companies to organize the directory using organization units (typically created along line-of-business boundaries) and then apply policies to each organizational unit individually. Rather than creating several domains that several domain controllers manage, they can create far fewer domains, divided into organizational units, with fewer domain controllers. Companies are already realizing dramatic TCO benefits.

For more information about Active Directory, see *http://www.microsoft.com*. Optionally, ask your IT department for a tour of Windows 2000 Server's directory service and let them wow you with its capabilities.

PRODUCTIVITY ENHANCEMENTS

Because Web Storage System enables users to access information using any client program, knowledge workers are more productive. Mechanically, opening the file you want with whatever client you happen to be using is quicker than exiting your current application and opening up a new one. Users can access information in Web Storage System using applications with which they are already familiar. For example, they can use tools like Office applications, Windows Explorer, or any Internet browser to find and edit information in Web Storage System.

The effect on TCO is immediate. The business does not have to retrain users, and administrators can take advantage of Web Storage System using skills they already possess. Training is not an issue. And because Web Storage System puts documents and applications in a single place, knowledge workers look in one place for documents, discussions, or any collaborative information. Also, administrators have only one technology to set up and administer but can provide users with the best collaborative solution to solve their business problems. Last, Web Storage System's native support for Internet protocols means that users can use any Internet-standard client to find and retrieve information. Support for two protocols, NNTP and SMTP, enables users to create and view newsgroup discussions as well as Internet-standard e-mail using Web Storage System.

Office 2000

Web Storage System enables Office 2000 users to store and retrieve documents within desktop applications such as Word. They can save documents directly into Web Storage System using the native File Save dialog box and can open them by using the File Open dialog box, two tools with which they should already be familiar. This enables users to leverage the security, replication, accessibility, and powerful workflow capabilities of Web Storage System as a repository for Office documents. Users can store all related information, e-mail messages, tasks, documents, or spreadsheets in a single folder and can access this folder from any client, including Windows Explorer, Outlook, Microsoft Outlook Express, or a Web browser.

An important characteristic of Web Storage System is its capability to store custom properties on the items stored in its database. Office users can leverage the power of Outlook to view, sort, and manage shared and personal documents with the same tools they currently use for e-mail, calendar, and contacts. The *property promotion* feature of Web Storage System provides a consistent view of information that is independent of the client used for access. Properties are automatically promoted from documents, populating all record fields like those for document author, title, and so on. Web Storage System shows different file types as entries; properties for each are promoted, and you can search across all your information, regardless of application type. Users can access this unified view of information in consistent ways across multiple clients. Accessing this unified view of information eliminates the need to open and close applications to view and access different types of data. It provides a view of all available user resources in one glance, enhancing productivity.

Outlook has always provided powerful replication features that work with Exchange Server so that knowledge workers can use collaborative information online and offline. With Windows 2000, they'll gain the benefit of synchroniz-ing file shares for use when disconnected from their network. This feature is *Offline Folders*, illustrated in Figure 8-4. With Web Storage System, any Windows 2000 user can take advantage of Offline Folders against a Web Storage System to synchronize the contents of that Web Storage System without having any specific client installed on their machine. Thus, by integrating with the Offline Folders feature, users can take advantage of a familiar replication model built into the operating system without any additional training by their IT department. Support for Offline Folders is indeed one of the greatest benefits of Web Storage System. Unlike the process before Web Storage System, users won't need to prepare to go offline by explicitly synchronizing folders and data. The process is transparent to them regardless of whether their applications are connected to or disconnected from the network. Collaborative applications become con-nection independent.

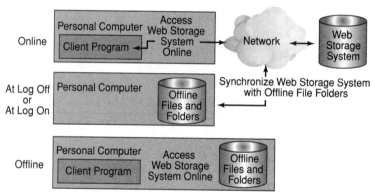

Figure 8-4. *Offline Folders.*

Collaboration Objects

Web Storage System provides out-of-the-box functionality for the most common collaboration scenarios, which include messaging, contacts, calendaring, and workflow. It provides an object model that developers can use to develop applications for Web Storage System. When combined with the powerful devel-opment tools that work with Web Storage System, this object model provides developers with an ideal collaborative development platform. Further, because these objects are integrated with the Web Storage System, developers do not have to create knock-off solutions for common scenarios, fueling rapid appli-cation development.

Development Tools

Web Storage System supports APIs such as OLE DB and ADO. As a result, it can leverage power development tools such as Microsoft Visual Studio, which makes developers more productive immediately without requiring training. And because Web Storage System supports Internet-based standards, developers can use tools like Microsoft FrontPage to develop Web-based applications for Web Storage System.

UNIFIED MESSAGING

Exchange Server and Web Storage System are at the heart of one of Microsoft's most ambitious initiatives: *unified messaging*. The goal of unified messaging, also known as a *messaging center*, is to provide a single place to access e-mail, voice mail, faxes, and pages, rather than using separate systems for each.

Just as important as a messaging center is the idea of *universal access*. That is, users can access their messages from any telephone, any online computer, or any combination of the two. Users have access to information anytime, anywhere. Microsoft extends this idea to include intelligent assistants, which automatically manage the knowledge worker's messaging center. Thus, Microsoft's definition of unified messaging is universal access to an intelligent messaging center able to manage e-mail, voice mail, faxes, and pages.

While Exchange Server is at the heart of unified messaging, providing some support for it already, other initiatives in this book also play key roles:

- **Digital Dashboard**   Enables users to manage their e-mail, voice mail, faxes, and pages through their digital dashboard see Chapter 7, "Digital Dashboard".

- **Wireless Solutions**   Enable universal access to users' messages by allowing them to access their mailboxes using wireless phones and similar devices see Chapter 9, "Wireless Solutions".

- **Intelligent Interfaces**   Provide intelligent assistants, the third part of Microsoft's vision for unified messaging see Chapter 10, "Intelligent Interfaces".

Exchange Server has started this process of evolution by providing a unified mailbox. All of the technology is not yet in place to make it a reality, however. And further in the future, Microsoft wants to eliminate the distinction between different types of technologies. Exactly how and on what media the system delivers a message will no longer be important. The system will just use what is most appropriate. In other words, a message will just be a message, no matter how it's delivered.

WRAP UP

Web Storage System, a new feature in Exchange 2000, provides knowledge workers a single place in which to store all information for a given topic. The type of document containing the information doesn't matter either, and users have access to it in any application they happen to be using at the time. Significant capabilities of Web Storage System include the following:

- Web Storage System provides a single database for messaging, collaboration, document storage, and Web-enabled applications.

- Numerous applications can access Web Storage System, including Outlook, Outlook Express, FrontPage, Office, Windows Explorer, any Web browser, or any other 32-bit application for Windows.

- Users can save Office documents directly to Web Storage System by using the File Save dialog box; also, they can open documents directly from Web Storage System.

- Users can access any item in Web Storage System by using a friendly address (URL) from their Web browser or from any other application.

- Web Storage System supports custom properties, enabling richer indexing, searching, and organization of documents within the database.

- Web Storage System includes built-in indexing to provide high-speed and accurate full-text searching, even within messages' attachments.

- Web Storage System supports DAV, a new protocol based on HTTP that enables people to collaborate on documents over the Web, regardless of the tools used to create the document.

- Developers can use XML to deliver structured data from other applications.

- Web Storage System supports scripting and ASP, enabling it to host Web pages.

- Administrators can store Web Storage System across multiple databases, enabling them to scale Web Storage System or make it more reliable by removing the single point of failure.

- Web Storage System fully integrates with Windows 2000 ACLs so that administrators grant or deny permissions one time by using a single user interface with which they're already familiar.

Taking Stock

1. How flexible is your company's infrastructure and standards?

2. Would your company benefit by storing all knowledge sources in one repository?

3. Does your company already use or is it planning to use Exchange Server?

4. Does your company already use or is it planning to use Office family products?

5. Have you identified the knowledge sources you want to put in Web Storage System?

6. Does your company have a development staff or a partner to extend Web Storage System?

7. Will your company deploy Windows 2000 Server and Active Directory so that it can take advantage of Web Storage System's integration with Windows 2000 security?

8. Will your company deploy Windows 2000 Professional so that users can take advantage of offline folders in conjunction with Web Storage System?

9. Have your company's administrators received training for Windows 2000?

10. Is load balancing, clustering, or replication important to your company?

11. Do you want administrators to be able to maintain complete control over usage for different groups of users, such as executives versus other workers?

ACTION PLAN

❑   Identify the knowledge sources you want to put in Web Storage System.

❑   Order a copy of Exchange Server 2000 and ask your IT staff to evaluate Web Storage System's position in your knowledge-management solution. If you're already using an earlier version of Exchange Server, start planning your upgrade.

❑   Ask your IT staff to create a deployment plan for Windows 2000 and make Windows 2000 training a priority for administrators and users.

❑   Create a deployment plan that includes information about deploying Web Storage System, moving knowledge sources into it, developing applications for it, and training users how to use and rely on it.

❑   Send key IT staff to deployment training for Windows 2000, Office 2000, and Exchange 2000 so that they'll be better able to plan. For more information about training, see *http://www.microsoft.com* or your Microsoft sales representative.

Chapter 9

Wireless Solutions

Wireless technology enables users to connect to your company's knowledge-management solution anytime, anywhere.

Recently, Microsoft changed its original vision, "A computer on every desk and in every home running Microsoft software," to a newer vision, "Connect anytime, anywhere." Read between the lines. This new vision means computers available all the time that connect you to the information you need no matter where you happen to be. The new millennium brings with it all of the exciting possibilities of ubiquitous computing and, true to Microsoft's form, the company will innovate in this arena like no other company can do. This chapter describes some of Microsoft's most exciting wireless innovations, most of which arise from partnering with third-party companies. The chapter then relates to you how that innovation affects your knowledge-management solutions in positive ways.

Microsoft's new vision forces it to think out-of-the-box about how your company delivers information. The most exciting results are wireless technologies that connect you to any source of information, particularly your company's knowledge-management portal, without any type of cable. As those airline commercials say, "You are free to move about the country." According to Microsoft, your company won't have to make significant changes to integrate wireless technologies, as long as it sticks with Internet-based standards. The devices that are available to your company vary from simple pagers and mobile phones to handheld computers. The challenge that Microsoft and its partners face is making these devices more intelligent and capable of talking to a network. Currently most mobile devices are limited to receiving asynchronous, unidirectional 150-character messages. But Microsoft plans to enable these devices to act like computers with built-in modems so that they can connect to wireless networks. To that end, Microsoft has developed technology called a *microbrowser* that allows users to view Web content on mobile devices, similar to how some mobile phones already allow you to do the same thing. You'll become familiar with the microbrowser by its new name: Microsoft Mobile Explorer.

Wireless technology is a reality, and you'll see more of it as cellular providers develop more data networks. Additionally, adapting Internet standards to wireless networks is a key factor in the success of companies trying to provide knowledge workers with access to any information anytime, anywhere. That's the job of the Wireless Application Protocol forum, which you also learn about in this chapter. As you read this chapter, don't think for a moment that these technologies are years down the road; far from it, wireless technology will be a reality for your company within the next year. That's why I suggest that, after reading this chapter, you ask your IT department to start investigating how to empower your knowledge workers with wireless technologies.

INDUSTRY STANDARDS

Organizations such as IETF (Internet Engineering Task Force), IEEE (Institute of Electrical and Electronics Engineers), and W3C (World Wide Web Consortium) define Internet protocols and data formats. These organizations receive very little credit for the fact that they've laid the foundations on which the Internet is built. Their standards revolutionized the telecommunications industry and are radically changing how companies build networks and develop applications. Rather than invent protocols and data formats specifically for wireless solutions, Microsoft is supporting wireless technology using the Internet standards that these groups defined. In this vein, the company is working with industry leadership to optimize existing protocols and data formats for wireless solutions.

Extending existing standards to support wireless solutions, instead of inventing new standards, is the best way to go. Wireless-only applications will be quite rare, according to Microsoft. Wireless solutions will extend the reach of server-based applications; therefore, companies must develop applications for both wired and wireless clients. Doing this efficiently means that those companies must use a single suite of standards and data formats to deliver seamless, interoperable applications for all clients and servers. Microsoft is proactively participating in the key standards setting organizations of the Internet. The goal of the company's participation is to ensure that a single, standard suite of Internet protocols and data representations are optimized for both wireless and wired networks.

Contrasting Microsoft's approach, the Wireless Application Protocol (WAP) forum is working on a suite of wireless-specific protocols and application-development profiles. (See the sidebar "Wireless Application Protocol Forum.") The forum's primary focus is delivery of wireless data to cellular phones. Microsoft isn't adopting this approach across the board because it doesn't use existing Internet standards to support broad ranges of interactive pagers, smart phones, handheld computers, desktop computers, and so on. The company *will* support WAP devices in its products, but Microsoft will also continue to support and encourage the use of standards such as HTML (HyperText Markup Language) and XML (Extensible Markup Language) at the application layer. What brings Microsoft to the WAP table is the work that the organization is doing in the transport and network layers to optimize wireless bandwidth.

Protocols

Microsoft is extending Microsoft Internet Information Server (IIS) to accommodate the use of the following Internet standard protocols for wireless applications:

- Header Conversion to negotiate sessions, track "session objects," and compress HTTP headers.

- Content Conversion to convert content from XML to HTML, filter HTML, and compress content based on the characteristics of a given client and the network.

- Push Features to implement new aspects of HTTP (HyperText Transfer Protocol) that provide true push capability. This feature is particularly important for wireless devices that provide paging-style message delivery.

Data Formats

Examples of specific data formats that Microsoft is focusing on include the following:

- **vCard**   vCard is a data format for exchanging business-card information. It defines a simple data format that describes how pieces of data (such as parts of a name, a title, a company, a phone number, a fax address, an e-mail address, a postal mail address, and so on) are exchanged on the Internet.

- **iCal**   iCal is similar to vCard, but iCal is a data format for exchanging calendar information. It uses a simple notation that Internet-based applications use to exchange data about appointments, events, and so on.

- **XML**   Extensible Markup Language (XML) is a recent W3C recommendation that's like HTML and SGML (Standard Generalized Markup Language) in that it defines a language for tagging information. XML is much more sophisticated than HTML or SGML because, rather than simply tagging text data for output, it's a general-purpose way to tag any type of structured data. That makes XML a universal data format that allows applications to appropriately search and render structured information.

WIRELESS APPLICATION PROTOCOL FORUM

Recently, the Wireless Application Protocol (WAP) forum and the World Wide Web Consortium (W3C) announced they were partnering to promote and define standards for wireless devices on the Web. They made this announcement during a WAP forum members meeting.

These two groups will define Web specifications that will enable wireless devices to access the Web. These specifications include testing and implementation processes. Also, they will promote these new specifications within the wireless industry. The bottom line of this collaboration is to enable people to use their mobile devices, particularly phones, to use data from the Internet and corporate intranets. The only drawback to the technology is that the WAP forum is developing standards that require special servers and administrators to control the content that is available to users. This is in sharp contrast to Microsoft's approach to wireless solutions, which relies on existing Internet standards to provide full access to the Internet and corporate intranets.

Although Microsoft is watching this group closely, the company doesn't buy into some of its philosophies. The biggest difference is the development of wireless-specific protocols. Microsoft believes that solutions must be network agnostic, allowing companies to deliver solutions to both network-connected and wireless devices. Doing so is best accomplished by extending *existing* Internet-based protocols for use by wireless applications, not inventing *new* protocols. What has Microsoft's attention is WAP's work in optimizing wireless throughput, a topic that promises to escalate over the next year as wireless broadband solutions hit the horizon. Even though Microsoft will continue to encourage the use of existing Internet protocols, it does plan to support WAP in many of its products.

WIRELESS CARRIERS

Huge varieties of wireless services are already available, and many more are now on the radar. Microsoft is partnering with wireless carriers to help them deploy wireless data services. The company will offer carriers numerous professional services, such as programs for integrating systems and certifying products. Microsoft plans to embark on a three-phase effort that includes trials with leading carriers, operators, and manufacturers; joint market development to build market awareness; and support of commercial deployment activities in Europe, the United States, and Asia by taking active roles in providing integration services. Microsoft will continue to seek new relationships with carriers, equipment manufacturers, application developers, and content providers as it identifies opportunities in wireless technology. Its joint venture with Qualcomm and *wireless*knowledge, LLC, is an example of the ventures that Microsoft is pursuing to ensure that the marketplace for wireless data solutions is available to your company as quickly as possible. For more information about this venture, see *http://www.wirelessknowledge.com.*

Recently, Eric Schultz, chairman and CEO of *wireless*knowledge, described how the market will drive the wireless services that are available. According to Schultz, demand is high for Short Message Service (SMS), which he equates to instant messaging for mobile phones and pagers. However, demand for SMS is coming more from individuals than from businesses. Business people will drive the next big demand for wireless services. They want tools such as wireless mobile devices to become their multifunction centers for communication. That means they want access to their e-mail, schedules, and other applications over their mobile phones.

Business is driving demand for the third type of service: wireless network bandwidth. As wireless bandwidth increases to 64K and beyond, businesses want to connect knowledge workers to their intranets. The final stage, which the industry has just started, is wireless connection of all of a business's devices to the Internet. The example that Schultz cites is a demonstration of the NTT Docomo I-MODE service (*http://www.nttdocomo.com/*), which uses existing Internet protocols to connect mobile devices to the Internet.

Network services include the communication infrastructure that allows clients and servers to connect with one another. In wireless configurations, only the *last mile* of the communication path ending with the client is wireless, and it uses one of the many available radio frequencies. The remainder of the network uses traditional networking and telecommunications technologies. The *first mile* of the communication path, beginning with the servers, is a LAN that your company operates or that a third-party service provider operates on your company's behalf. Everything between the first and last miles might be exclusively data networks, voice and data networks, or voice networks carrying modulated data to a modem. Your wireless solution will undoubtedly include partnerships with wireless service providers. A good place to start your search for those providers is at Microsoft's ISN Web site, *http://www.microsoft.com/isn*. Microsoft publishes this Web site for wireless service providers, and the case studies, press releases, and other information on this site can quickly lead you to a service provider that matches your requirements. Another source for locating service providers is the Microsoft Certified Solution Provider (MCSP) program about which you learned in this book's introduction.

MICROSOFT PRODUCTS

For wireless solutions, Microsoft offers server products, client products, and development tools. The company emphasizes its end-to-end support, providing one-stop shopping for companies deploying new wireless solutions or upgrading existing solutions. Customers can take advantage of Microsoft's range of products that are optimized for specific clients and servers. For example, Microsoft is pursuing varieties of opportunities to build wireless data service centers, deliver Microsoft-branded content to wireless subscribers, develop applications for wireless devices, assist companies building wireless solutions, and partner with manufacturers to develop new wireless devices.

The following Microsoft products are useful for building wireless solutions (you learn more about how Microsoft products might fit into your wireless solutions in the following sections):

Server Products
- Microsoft Windows 2000 Server
- Microsoft Internet Information Server (IIS)
- Microsoft BackOffice Server

Developer Tools
- Microsoft FrontPage
- Microsoft Visual InterDev
- Microsoft Visual Basic
- Microsoft Visual C++
- Microsoft Visual J++

Client Software	■	Microsoft Windows 2000 Professional
	■	Microsoft Windows 98
	■	Microsoft Windows CE
	■	Microsoft Outlook 2000
	■	Microsoft Internet Explorer

Client Devices

Traditionally, client-server solutions include a user interface on a desktop computer and an application hosted on a server. However, numerous microprocessor-equipped devices capable of acting as clients are booming onto the scene. As these client devices get smaller, they become mobile. This diversity of small mobile devices is making the move to wireless networking inevitable. Client devices in wireless solutions range from the ubiquitous laptop computers to handheld organizers to cellular phones. As devices get smaller, less space is available on the screen, and I/O is simpler. Effective wireless solutions must deliver applications and data to the entire spectrum of client devices.

As client devices get smaller, those built on Microsoft technologies have key attributes that make them suitable for wireless solutions:

■ **Instant On**—All of the operating system software and core applications are protected in a read-only memory (ROM) chip. Immediate access to applications and data gives these devices the convenience of paper.

■ **Small Devices**—Handheld computers are small, are lightweight, and have tiny screens. Cellular phones are even smaller, are even lighter, and can display even less content than handheld computers, typically text only.

■ **Long Battery Life**—Windows CE supports more than 20 low-power CPUs. The small size of the operating system, in conjunction with these lower-power CPUs, enables these devices to conserve battery power. A typical mobile device can last all day on a single charge.

■ **Synchronization**—Microsoft ActiveSync technology enables users to keep data synchronized between their mobile devices and desktop computers. This includes users' calendars, contact information, e-mail messages, task lists, files, and databases.

■ **Developer Support**—Windows CE retains the key elements of the Win32 Application Programming Interface (API). As a result, developers can leverage their existing expertise to develop wireless applications for Windows CE.

In support of client devices for wireless solutions, Microsoft is investing a lot of energy in Windows CE. When properly implemented, this operating system and the tools that come with it can be the heart and soul of any company's wireless solution. For more information about Windows CE, see the section "Windows CE" later in this chapter.

Data and Applications

Without access to users' own data, wireless applications are no better than the news broadcasts and stock quotes that pagers receive. Users want wireless access to their information, which can include address books; a universal mailbox that contains e-mail messages, faxes, and voice mail messages; task lists; personal calendars; and important documents. Access to this type of information is essential to any personal digital assistant. The ability to exchange e-mail, access the Internet, and connect to the corporate intranet are essential to wireless solutions, too. It's all about connecting knowledge workers to knowledge sources where and when they need them.

Organizations can take advantage of wireless technology to move their knowledge workers into the field, where they are most beneficial to the business, while fostering *anytime, anywhere* work styles among their employees. To do so, organizations must make their mission-critical data, applications, and processes available to remote and mobile users. Organizational data includes structured data, such as customer databases, price lists, corporate directories, inventory databases, and accounting data. It also includes unstructured data, such as product data, project schedules, media libraries, news archives, and so on. Beyond raw data itself are the automated business processes and applications that provide useful access to these databases.

Microsoft provides software for a wide range of wireless client devices. Laptop computers running Microsoft Windows 98 or Microsoft Windows 2000 Professional can connect to server applications on a variety of networks. Microsoft Outlook 2000 connects users to Microsoft Exchange servers. Internet Explorer is a client that connects to IIS and other Web servers. Smaller client devices can use Windows CE and its suite of client applications to connect to Exchange servers as well as Web servers. The obvious trade-off between using laptop and handheld computers is that laptop computers can provide richer access to your knowledge management solutions while handheld computers can provide more convenient wireless access to the company's sources of information.

To offset the trade-offs between each type of vehicle, many knowledge workers use both types of devices. For example, field salespeople might use their wireless handheld devices to quickly check their e-mail while taking a taxicab from the airport to their hotel. At customers' sites, however, they might use their laptop computers to connect wirelessly to their companies' product databases and ordering systems during their sales calls. The night before big pitches, they might use their laptop computers to connect to their knowledge portals and extract information that's important to their presentations. Then they could store important notes and excerpts on their handheld devices for immediate access to the information. They use their laptop computers when they need richer access to information, and they use their handheld devices when they need quicker, immediate access to simpler forms of information.

Development Tools

As Microsoft is doing for industry standards, the company is extending its application platform to wireless solutions instead of creating application platforms specific to the wireless world. This approach allows companies to deploy existing applications to new generations of wireless devices. It also allows companies to build wireless applications using tools with which they're already familiar and easily develop applications that work in wired and wireless domains. To be fair, your company isn't limited to using development tools from Microsoft. Your developers can continue to use the tools in which you've already invested significant chunks of your budget. Thus, companies can quickly focus their existing development tools and talent on delivering applications and services for wireless users.

For example, Hoechst Marion Roussel (HMR), an international pharmaceutical manufacturer, has more than 1500 sales representatives who call on an average of 8 to 10 physicians every day. Because physicians are busy people, HMR representatives estimate that they have anywhere from 45 seconds to 10 minutes with a physician to present their products and leave samples. In searching for ways to speed up the process, the company's IS staff chose Windows CE-based handheld computers, as they offered several advantages. One advantage was that Windows CE offers a number of benefits from a developer's perspective. Because it is based on the familiar Win32 API and its development tools are extensions to the standard Win32 tools, it requires only a short learning curve. Its enormous flexibility allowed HMR developers to meet very specific requirements for speed, screen customization, and functionality. "Windows CE is very close to the normal Win32 development platform, so it was a pretty small learning curve," notes developer Jamie Hohman.

Windows CE is the operating system on the handheld computers that many companies choose for their wireless solutions, and it uses a subset of the same APIs that are in Microsoft's bigger 32-bit operating systems. The result is the developers are already familiar with the libraries they need to create best-of-breed applications for wireless devices running Windows CE. Windows CE extends devices that were designed to be wired so they can support wireless connectivity. When developing applications that run on Windows CE, developers can continue to use Microsoft tools, such as Visual C++, Visual InterDev, and even their favorite text editor for editing HTML. Developers can also continue to use FrontPage to prepare content for Windows CE. They must be aware of the limitations in the devices' Web browsers, however. For example, Mobile Explorer, the microbrowser that Microsoft is developing for smart phones (see the section "Smart Phones"), supports only a subset of HTML tags.

Server Products

Servers make data and applications available to client devices. They are more powerful and more cost effective now than at any time in history. That trend will only continue as Intel increases the power of its processors and as Microsoft continues the track it's on with Windows 2000 Server, the foundation for Microsoft's wireless solutions. Of Microsoft's operating systems for servers, Windows 2000 Server is the easiest to use, and the company designed it for demanding businesses. It includes integrated networking, application, and communication services. An essential part of Windows 2000 Server is Internet Information Server (IIS). IIS provides the ability to support Web-based applications on the server and to deliver Web content to Web-based clients. IIS not only supports the applications that provide access to live content and generate dynamic Web pages, but it also includes an API that supports low-level plug-ins to extend the server in new ways. Other key services in Windows 2000 Server include Index Server, Windows Terminal Server, message queuing, and transaction processing.

For example, the IIS extensions you read about in the section "Protocols" are actually extensions implemented as ISAPI components. (ISAPI is an interface that allows programmers to develop extensions that work as a part of IIS.) Microsoft is developing the Wireless Access Services as IIS filters, which allows third-party companies to extend IIS by using established interfaces. Examples of other extensions to IIS include the following:

- Common user and device session management, as well as a common session object that includes authentication, user preferences, and device capabilities.

- Session content generation. Some clients can parse XML while others might require HTML. This extension provides the ability to automatically produce the richest content the client can handle. It also includes the ability to reformat HTML content for better representation on the client.

- Notification services with the capability to establish peer-to-peer push channels.

- Data synchronization services to synchronize information and data, such as favorites, cookies, and other settings.

For more information about using Microsoft server products in your wireless knowledge-management solutions, see Chapter 7, "Digital Dashboard," and Chapter 8, "Exchange Web Storage System."

WINDOWS CE

Microsoft Windows CE is an operating system that enables a broad range of handheld, mobile devices. Windows CE is a 32-bit, multitasking, multithreaded operating system that Microsoft built using proven design concepts found in other versions of Windows. OEMs shipped the first products based on Windows CE, handheld computers, in 1996. Windows CE is now available in a full range of products, including pocket PCs, digital pagers, and cellular smart phones. You can even find Windows CE in a range of consumer appliances, such as game consoles, DVD players, digital set-top boxes, and so on. The most exciting development in Windows CE is its support for wireless solutions and the new features in Windows CE 2.1. Windows CE 2.1 is the most recent version of the mobile operating system; it enhances version 2, adding incremental changes to existing features. It supports more types of hardware, has more database APIs, and includes COM capabilities. These and other changes make it better resemble desktop versions of Windows. For example, it supports cryptography, file systems and thread handling, and localization.

Examples of how your company can use wireless devices running Windows CE include the following:

- **Sales Force Automation**—Expecting to save approximately $5 million annually, Hoechst Marion Roussel, a global pharmaceutical company, equipped its sales representatives with handheld PCs.

Representatives can now quickly capture sample-drug distribution details, including physicians' signatures, and exchange customer background and sales information with the company's headquarters.

- **Reliable Two-Way Messaging**—Goldman Sachs uses Windows CE-based devices to keep track of current information about the market for particular securities. The company's IT organization developed an application that connects the wireless infrastructure of the New York Stock Exchange to Goldman Sachs' existing trading systems.

- **Secure Wireless Communication**—Paradigm4, a Microsoft Solution Provider, developed an application for the Pittsburgh Police Department that provides secure access to data officers need while they're on patrol. This data includes the city's warrant information, the state's vehicle registrations and driver licenses, and national crime databases.

- **Geographic Information Systems**—The U.S. Marines use handheld devices to extend their Command and Control system, communicating orders as well as geographic information about enemy positions.

Snyder Healthcare Sales's clients are some of the biggest names in the pharmaceutical industry. The company recognized the need for digital systems that are faster and more accurate than its aging and inefficient paper-based sales system. After plenty of soul searching, the company decided to use handheld computers based on Windows CE, along with a custom application to automate the paper-based processes its sales force had been using. The company, which started deployment in the summer of 1998, is reaping benefits by delivering accurate data to clients much faster than before. According to Snyder, the accuracy rate for sales data collected on behalf of its customers has jumped to 100 percent, up from 85 to 90 percent with its paper-based processes. The time it takes Snyder to provide reports to its clients has dropped from 60 days or longer after a sales call to just 10 days. "The bottom line is that we can provide far better service to our customers, which lets them make decisions faster and gives us an edge on our competition," says Tom Pollock, senior director of information systems at Snyder. "By moving to the Windows CE-based technology, we've eliminated a lot of internal headaches that we had using paper."

BLUETOOTH

On the forefront of wireless technology is Bluetooth. At COMDEX in the fall of 1999, Bluetooth stole the show by introducing technology that enables low-cost wireless communications and networking. Within Bluetooth's domain are portable and desktop computers; mobile phones and pagers; and a whole host of connected devices that we don't even know about yet.

Bluetooth created the Bluetooth Special Interest Group (SIG) to deliver products based on Bluetooth technologies. It includes several companies, and Microsoft is prominently featured in that list. Microsoft's interest in Bluetooth is to further its vision of connecting users to their data anytime, anywhere. Microsoft is evaluating Bluetooth technology as part of its long-term strategy for building what Microsoft calls personal area networks. Part of its attraction includes ad hoc networking, support of Universal Plug and Play, and so on. Microsoft expects that participating in these innovations will expand its ability to ship new wireless solutions to users.

Microsoft's role in the Bluetooth SIG is not as an adopter. Microsoft is participating as a promoter, which means that the company will work with industry leaders to promote the technology. The company will actively participate in working groups and provide marketing, public relations, and regulatory help.

MOBILE EXPLORER

The cellular smart phone and digital pager are emerging client devices that Microsoft is targeting for Windows CE. These low-end devices don't have enough resources to run generic applications, but they do have software-driven user interfaces, displays, and sufficient input capabilities to make them capable of providing wireless access to data. To enable these devices to connect knowledge workers to the information they need, anytime, anywhere, Microsoft is developing the microbrowser and defining a lightweight client architecture based on it. This will support all the protocols and data types described in this chapter, making it a universal, wireless-optimized client for Web applications.

The microbrowser is independent of any operating system. It uses an Operating System Abstraction Layer to hide operating-system details. When the microbrowser calls an operating-system service, it uses one of the abstraction layer's well-defined APIs instead of calling the operating system directly; the microbrowser filters all operating-system access through this abstraction layer. This approach, which is similar to Windows 2000's hardware-abstraction layer, allows

OEMs to port the microbrowser to different operating systems by simply creating an abstraction layer for the different system. As part of the Wireless Product Adaptation Kit (WPAK), Microsoft is also making the microbrowser's source code available to OEMs to enable open solutions. The WPAK contains the following:

- Source code for the Windows CE microbrowser

- Customizable code for the user interface

- Details about the Operating System Abstraction Layer

- Sample code, libraries, and documentation

Microbrowser technology is compatible with the full range of Internet standards. It supports HTTP 1.1, HTML 3.2, and telephone integration using the *tel:* protocol designator for URLs. It has a well-defined event model that it expresses through XML and includes a real-time notification engine. The Operating System Abstraction Layer includes APIs for security, networking, storage, memory management, display, input, and telephony control. The storage API is an abstraction layer, which can map to a local store or the server, depending on the capability of the device. Capabilities for synchronizing information and data in the local store with that on the server is provided through standard formats, including vCard and iCal.

You'll recognize microbrowser technology in its current incarnation as Microsoft Mobile Explorer. This is a platform for mobile phones that enables secure access to corporate data, e-mail, the Internet, and electronic-commerce applications from feature and smart phones. Knowledge workers can have access to the information they need, anytime, anywhere. You learn more about Mobile Explorer in the following sections.

Feature Phones

Mobile Explorer for feature phones is a wireless-telephone browser solution capable of running networked applications. It gives mobile users quick and easy access to e-mail messages, calendar data, contact information, voice-mail messages, and the Internet while connected to their Internet service providers or carriers/operators.

Mobile Explorer for feature phones is operating-system independent and works on any wireless network. This microbrowser supports HTML-standard Web content as well as Wireless Markup Language (WML), which complies with the Wireless Applications Protocol (WAP) version 1.1. Mobile Explorer provides a global standard for Internet access through handheld devices such as cellular phones. By supporting both of these standards, Mobile Explorer for feature phones lets carriers offer a choice of content and services to their customers, and it gives users a great online experience. It allows these companies to offer their customers a browser that supports graphics, cookies, favorites, and forms. The browser also links to phone-specific applications so that users can dial phone numbers directly from a Web site (if the site uses the *tel:* protocol designator for URLs).

The first version of Mobile Explorer for feature phones is currently in carrier trials. Microsoft is scheduled to make version 2 available by the second quarter of 2000. This version will include additional support for robust and secure corporate access, e-mail, personal information access, as well as dual mode HTML and WAP 1.1-based Internet access.

Smart Phones

Mobile Explorer for smart phones is a mobile phone solution that runs both networked and local software. Based on the application-rich Windows CE operating system, Mobile Explorer for smart phones gives mobile phone users a high-resolution display and access to a suite of local applications, including their calendars, contact software, task lists, a graphical Web browser, and a media player. With a cellular phone based on Mobile Explorer for smart phones, knowledge workers can conduct many of the same tasks they perform at a desktop PC; these tasks include reading and replying to e-mail and voice-mail messages, using contact lists to manage calls and customer visits, reviewing tasks and notes, and browsing the Web.

Mobile Explorer for smart phones includes an Inbox application for managing written communication and a utility for managing voice-mail messages. This lets a user easily manage both e-mail and SMS messages. Phones sporting Mobile Explorer for smart phones also support advanced voice-communication features, such as integration with personal data when sending and receiving calls. Mobile Explorer for smart phones also provides a graphical Web browser, with Web content displayed on a high-resolution color screen. This enables customers to easily navigate links, select services, and enter URLs. The secure Web browser will also enable e-commerce and other transaction-based services.

Because it runs applications locally and over a network, Mobile Explorer for smart phones will let knowledge workers stay connected to their data, anytime, anywhere. Synchronization is automatic and seamless, so the mobile phone reflects the current state of the users' data. They can instantly access up-to-date information while offline from their wireless services. Alternatively they can remain connected to their data, with the wireless data link offering a continuous communication channel to the customer's data sources.

Carrier trials of Mobile Explorer for smart phones have already started. Microsoft is scheduled to release it to OEMs by the middle of 2000.

WRAP UP

A key technology that enables knowledge workers to access the information they need anytime, anywhere is wireless connectivity. Exciting, new wireless technologies are making their ways on to the radar screen, some from Microsoft and some from third-party companies.

- Rather than inventing wireless standards, Microsoft intends to work with standards bodies to enhance existing standards for use with wireless networks.

- The Wireless Application Protocol (WAP) forum is defining wireless specific standards for delivering content to wireless devices, but this technology does not integrate well with companies' existing infrastructure.

- Microsoft is expanding Internet Information Server (IIS) for wireless applications. The company is also targeting data formats such as XML in its products.

- Wireless-service providers are ramping up broad ranges of services that are useful for any company's knowledge-management solution, ranging from Short Message Service (SMS) to broadband wireless service.

- Client devices suitable for wireless solutions have the following characteristics: they turn on instantly, they are very small units, they have extended battery life, they synchronize with users' network data, and they allow developers to leverage their existing knowledge on a platform for wireless computing.

- Developing applications for Windows CE requires the same knowledge as does developing for other 32-bit versions of Windows, allowing developers to use tools and APIs with which they are already familiar.

- Windows CE is the heart and soul of Microsoft's wireless initiatives. Variations of Windows CE, such as Mobile Explorer for smart phones, enable a full range of wireless solutions on devices such as digital pagers and cellular phones.

Taking Stock

1. Would your company's knowledge workers benefit from wireless access to information?

2. Are laptop computers a suitable client device for your company's wireless users?

3. Are handheld computers based on Windows CE a suitable client device for your company's wireless users?

4. Are mobile phones based on Mobile Explorer the best client device for your company's wireless users?

5. Will you use wireless devices as they are out of the box or will your company require them to be customized by your IT department or a third party?

6. Is your IT department able to develop wireless applications?

7. Does your infrastructure use Internet standards? If not, is your IT department prepared to deploy Internet standards such as TCP/IP?

8. What does your company hope to accomplish with its wireless solution? Access to a knowledge-management portal? E-mail? Internet access? Calendaring?

9. Of the knowledge sources that your company has identified, which of these sources do you want to deliver to wireless users in the field?

10. If your company doesn't use Microsoft server products, is your current vendor focusing on your need for wireless solutions in its product development plan?

11. Have you identified a service provider for wireless access to your intranet?

ACTION PLAN

❑ Make sure that you can communicate to your IT department an overall vision for how your wireless solutions must fit with your knowledge-management strategies.

❑ Deploy server products that use Internet standards and that can take advantage of wireless technologies as they develop.

❑ Choose a wireless service provider that can connect wireless client devices to your network. See *http://www.microsoft.com/isn* for help making this choice.

---

continued

Action Plan *continued*

- ❑ Select the types of wireless client devices your company will use and the groups of users to which you will deploy each type of device.

- ❑ Develop the wireless applications your company wants to deploy. An example is a knowledge-management portal designed for wireless clients.

- ❑ Pilot your wireless devices and applications with a cross section of users.

- ❑ Deploy the company's wireless devices to the appropriate groups of users, and train them appropriately. Many users will require no training at all.

Chapter 10

Intelligent Interfaces

Microsoft is developing intelligent interfaces that will change the way users interact with their computers; keyboards just might be a thing of the past.

So far in this book, you've read about Microsoft's more substantive knowledge-management initiatives, including Digital Dashboard and Microsoft Exchange Web Storage System. Microsoft's most recent initiative is further thinking. According to Rich Tong, vice president of the Business Productivity Group at Microsoft, the company is betting that "we can significantly change the way people interact with computers." The company is making big investments in speech technology, natural language processing, and more. You don't see the full scope of this technology on your desktop today, but major breakthroughs are on the radar screen. Microsoft recently transferred a large part of its research group to its product groups, which is "a symbol of what we expect will happen," according to Tong.

This chapter briefly describes key areas that Microsoft is researching. The company does not guarantee that it will deliver all of these technologies. And, as this technology reaches further into the future than Microsoft's other initiatives, many details are missing. Regardless, intelligent interfaces promise to make computing resources more accessible and more convenient for all knowledge workers, and this chapter gives you a sneak peak. All of the case studies you've seen in this book have one theme in common: easy-to-use, standard user interfaces are key ingredients in any knowledge-management solution. Intelligent interfaces will make already effective knowledge portals even easier to use. Intelligent interfaces allow knowledge workers to interact with computers in natural, human ways, rather than using paradigms forced on them by years of computing baggage.

USER INTERFACES

Microsoft is exploring varieties of three-dimensional user interfaces that help users visualize information in new ways. The company is looking for new ways to help users navigate and ways to provide more information space on a small desktop. Microsoft is researching methods for replacing the current two-dimensional desktops with three-dimensional desktops, for example, which are more interesting and allow users to display more information in a similar area.

The following are a couple of examples of what Microsoft is researching, and you can find more information about these topics in the following sections:

- **Persona** Conversational assistants that help users complete tasks.

- **Task Gallery** Extensions of the desktop metaphor that turn the screen into a room in which users work. Along the walls of the room, which is a gallery, users see paintings that represent different tasks.

Persona

Microsoft Research's Persona project is researching technologies that create conversational assistants: lifelike animated characters that interact with users using natural spoken dialogue. It uses the Whisper speaker-independent continuous speech-recognition system and a broad-coverage English understanding system, which you learn about later in this chapter. In Microsoft's initial prototype, which you might have seen in some of the company's television commercials, an expressive three-dimensional parrot named Peedy responds to users' requests for music. For example, when a user asks Peedy, "What albums do you have from Madonna?" it scans through its database (see the section "Data Retrieval" later in this chapter) and responds, "I have *The Immaculate Collection* from 1990." Also, Peedy uses humanlike mannerisms to express itself. For example, if Peedy doesn't understand a user's request, it might raise its wing to its ear and ask, "What?" Additionally, varieties of sound effects and cinematic camera techniques support the conversation.

TaskGallery

Microsoft Windows' current user interface uses the familiar metaphor of a desktop to help users organize their work. The desktop was a major breakthrough when it first replaced the MS-DOS command-line prompt some two decades ago, making computers accessible to more people. Now, Microsoft believes that the time has come for the company to start working on the next step forward, which it believes will help users deal with the ever-increasing amount of information they must manage every day.

Microsoft's TaskGallery is a three-dimensional user interface that expands the electronic desktop into an entire office with an unlimited number of desktops. (Think *virtual desktops* with a three-dimensional twist.) The screen becomes a three-dimensional gallery with paintings hanging on the walls, with each painting a representation of a different task. Users move quickly from one task to another using the mouse or the keyboard. Microsoft Research is trying to relate the illusion to lessons that children learn about physical space so that users *get* the system intuitively without having to learn or adjust to it. Placement of tasks in TaskGallery takes advantage of users' spatial memory; the active task takes center stage on a platform at the end of the room, and other tasks are in the periphery. Users can arrange tasks any way they want, and the system will remember the tasks' organization. Users quickly switch between any task using the mouse or the keyboard.

SPEECH RECOGNITION

For some users, speech recognition is the best way to interact with computers. And, according to Microsoft, speech recognition promises to be the dominant human-computer interface in the near future. Microsoft quotes Gartner Group's prediction that speech recognition will be integrated into mainstream operating systems by 2002, for example. Deloitte & Touche Consulting surveyed more than a thousand chief executives in health care organizations. Of those polled, 40 percent plan to use speech recognition within the next two years. Even though you might have heard a lot of negative spin about speech recognition, particularly from technology reviewers, the technology is advancing at a rapid pace. Microsoft's $45 million investment in Lernout and Hauspie, (*http://www.lhs.com*) a leader in speech-recognition technology, is an indication of Microsoft's commitment to build speech recognition into the company's products.

Most users are familiar with speech-recognition applications based on dictation grammars, also known as continuous speech recognition, or have at the very least read one of the many negative reviews of this technology. It requires large commitments from users, who have to spend time training the speech-recognition engine and learning to speak in a consistent drone to assure a high degree of accuracy. Most users won't commit enough time and energy to the process and don't use the technology successfully as a result. Instead, users want to sit down and start using a product without having to train it or themselves. Other forms of speech recognition are eliminating the need for training, however.

Look for two kinds of speech recognition to appear in Microsoft products over the next few years:

- **Dictation**   This type of speech recognition allows users to speak continuously while the computer converts their spoken words into text. For example, a lawyer might use speech recognition to create a letter without using a keyboard.

- **Command and Control**   This type of speech recognition allows users to issue commands using speech, rather than a keyboard and mouse. An example is a user telling a word processor to delete a sentence by saying, "Delete the last sentence."

Microsoft is proactively refining its Speech Application Programming Interface (SAPI) and is making it available to developers wanting to speech-enable their applications. Speech recognition is also showing itself in Microsoft applications. The most notable is Microsoft Encarta, the company's world-class encyclopedia. Users can search for articles by using plain English, spoken queries such as, "What city is the capital of Texas?" Auto PC is another Microsoft product that uses speech recognition to give users hands-free access to information. As users drive their cars, they can ask for directions, check their e-mail, or change radio channels by issuing spoken commands rather than taking their hands off of the steering wheel. For more information, see Microsoft's Intelligent Interface Technologies site, *http://www.microsoft.com/iit*.

TEXT-TO-SPEECH

Text-to-speech is a process through which text is rendered as digital audio and then spoken by the computer. Text-to-speech is most appropriate in two scenarios in which audio files are not feasible: an audio file is too large to store on disk or creating an audio file is impossible because its contents are not known ahead of time. Practical uses for text-to-speech that Microsoft identifies include the following:

- **Reading Dynamic Text**   Text-to-speech is useful for phrases that vary too much to record. Speaking the time is a good example in which storing all the possible combinations of time is impractical.

- **Proofreading**   Audibly proofreading text and numbers helps users catch typing errors missed by visual proofreading (it's a fresh set of *ears*) for proofreading.

- **Conserving Storage Space**   Text-to-speech is useful for phrases that would occupy too much storage space if they were prerecorded in digital-audio format.

- **Notifying the User of Events**   Text-to-speech is useful for informational messages. Narrator, which comes with Microsoft Windows 2000, is a good example of a feature that helps people with visual disabilities better navigate. To inform users that print jobs are complete, for example, applications can say "Printing complete" rather than displaying a message and requiring users to click OK.

- **Providing Audible Feedback**   Text-to-speech can provide audible feedback when visual feedback is inadequate or difficult. For example, users' eyes might be busy with other tasks, such as transcribing data from a paper document. Users who have poor vision might rely on text-to-speech for feedback.

Text-to-speech is nothing new, but Microsoft's innovations make the results more natural. The company's new text-to-speech engine includes new and better voices (female, male, and robotic), and it handles text normalization better, making the results sound a bit more normal. You can sample Microsoft's text-to-speech engine in Windows 2000 using Narrator, which is the accessibility tool that reads text to users who have visual disabilities. Look for additional Microsoft tools, including Internet Explorer, to support text-to-speech in the future.

DATA RETRIEVAL

Microsoft SQL Server 7 includes a feature that is important to building intelligent interfaces, one that integrates with other Microsoft initiatives, such as speech recognition, to allow users to find information using natural spoken language. The feature is English Query. It allows users to retrieve data from a database by asking questions in plain English. Figure 10-1 on the following page shows how English Query interacts with applications and SQL Server 7. As shown, users ask a plain-English question such as, "Who lives in Boston?" and the English Query Engine uses the English Query Application's knowledge about the database and its semantics to generate the SQL statement. The client application can then use the SQL statement to query the database and retrieve the results for the user.

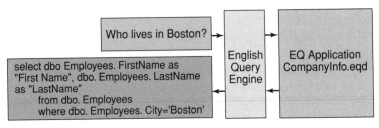

Figure 10-1. *English Query.*

Without speech recognition, users must type their queries, but with speech recognition, they can search using spoken words. By using English Query and speech recognition together, developers can provide users the ability to ask questions about a data source almost as naturally as they would ask another person. This provides a distinct advantage for supporting visually impaired users, users who suffer from repetitive motion disorders, and users with other disabilities.

WRAP UP

Microsoft's intelligent interface initiatives will make computers easier to use for all knowledge workers, eventually eliminating the requirement for keyboards and pointing devices. The result will be smaller, more portable devices that knowledge workers can use on the go and control with the spoken word. The initiatives you read about in this chapter include the following:

- Microsoft is investigating new user interfaces for computers that include animated assistants and three-dimensional spaces in which users can organize their tasks.

- Speech recognition promises to make computers easier to use, because users can interact with the computer in more natural ways than using a keyboard. Speech recognition is particularly important for the future of handheld devices, as these devices won't have keyboards as they become smaller and more generic.

- Text-to-speech provides an alternative way for users to absorb information, by hearing it read aloud. For example, users can *listen* to their e-mail rather than reading it.

- SQL Server 7's English Query and speech recognition make an exciting combination that allows users to search for information using spoken requests such as, "What is the company's best-selling product today?"

Taking Stock

1. Is your IT department ready for new advances when they become available?

2. How open is your organization to technology advances such as three-dimensional desktops, animated assistants, and speech recognition?

3. Is your IT department proactively tracking initiatives such as speech recognition and natural language processing?

4. In what ways can you envision your organization using intelligent interfaces?

ACTION PLAN

❑ List and prioritize the types of human-computer interactions that you can improve using the intelligent interfaces you learned about in this chapter.

❑ Keep current with the latest intelligent interface technology by frequenting Microsoft's Web site, *http://www.microsoft.com/iit*.

Part IV

Appendix

Appendix

Technology Roadmap

This appendix is a technology roadmap that helps you evaluate and build a comprehensive knowledge-management solution. Not only does it help you identify a knowledge-management solution's modules, but it also helps you evaluate the successful implementation of each module. This appendix is not a development plan or design. Read it with the intention of learning how a typical knowledge-management solution built with Microsoft products might look in your organization. Read it so that you can better communicate with your IT organization and communicate your requirements to them.

When Microsoft developed this roadmap, it faced several challenges. Knowledge management was and is still not well understood from a technological or an organizational standpoint. Also, the industry doesn't have a commonly accepted definition of knowledge-management features, with the exception of collaboration, workflow, and automating information flow such as e-mail. As a result, this isn't an academic approach to knowledge management such as you'll find in many textbooks. It's a pragmatic approach to understanding the technology in a typical knowledge-management system in the real world.

ENABLING MODULES

For each business problem in a company, knowledge management evolves through choosing the right technologies depending on the problems that the company needs to solve. Each company has its own characteristics based on organizational processes and technologies. This appendix describes each of the modules, shown in Figure A-1, of knowledge management and defines the organizational requirements and technologies that need to be implemented to enable an infrastructure with knowledge-management services.

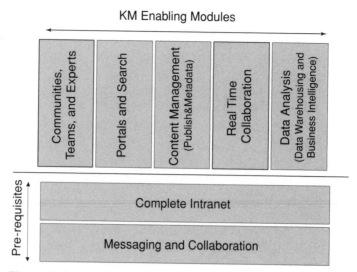

Figure A-1. *Knowledge-management modules.*

Two modules are prerequisites. An intranet and a messaging system form the foundation of any knowledge-management system, and they constitute an infrastructure that supports the efficient transport, structure, access, and collaborative management of electronic data. The remaining enabling modules extend that basic infrastructure to a sophisticated knowledge-management system that includes services like Content Management, variations of Information Delivery, and Data Analysis. Automated services such as Data Tracking and Workflow Processes are also included as part of the Community and Team modules.

The implementation of the enabling modules has a true plug-and-play character. Although some of the modules profit from the implementation of a previous module, they can be added in any order related to the specific business need that you're trying to meet. For example, Real-Time Collaboration services, such as video conferencing, can be easily included on top of the prerequisite technologies, but they are enhanced by the Metadata services provided in the Content Management Module.

Microsoft's KM Platform

The knowledge-management platform's modules provide great knowledge-management systems with broad support. The knowledge-management platform offers a typical, but extended, three-layered architecture that allows your company to build a flexible, powerful, and scaleable knowledge-management solution. Figure A-2 shows these three layers, and the following list describes them in more detail:

■ The *Knowledge Desktop* layer consists of familiar productivity tools, such as Microsoft Office, and integrates tightly with the Knowledge Services layer.

■ The *Knowledge Services* layer provides important knowledge-management services such as collaboration, document management, and search and deliver functionality, with modules for Tracking, Workflow, and Data Analysis.

■ The *System* layer is a foundation that includes administration, security, and directories for managing the knowledge-management platform. All services run on the System layer and benefit from the integrated communication services that connect with external solutions, platforms, and partners.

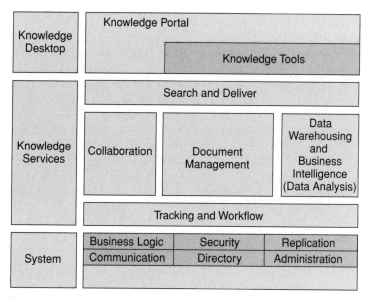

Figure A-2. *Layers of a knowledge-management platform.*

The Microsoft knowledge-management platform relies on the Microsoft BackOffice family of products, which provide the services you need to build the knowledge-management prerequisites (messaging and collaboration and complete intranet) and to extend those prerequisites into knowledge-management solutions by implementing all five knowledge-management enabling modules

(Content Management, Communities and Teams, Portals and Search, Data Analysis, and Real-Time Collaboration). Besides these services, BackOffice provides interfaces for connecting to and integrating with legacy information or knowledge sources, such as RDBMS systems, SNA data sources, or knowledge-management enabling technologies such as Lotus Notes or Lotus Domino. Figure A-3 illustrates how Microsoft technologies map to the layers of the knowledge-management platform you saw in Figure A-2.

One of the great advantages of BackOffice is the ability to migrate its services from a single server or to multiple servers without experiencing a major change in services or security aspects. This provides a platform that is scalable without the need for changes in the solutions that run on top of BackOffice. This ability is especially relevant to departmental server solutions where Lotus Notes and Lotus Domino provide a common groupware platform. There, BackOffice extends the departmental groupware functionalities with its integrated and scaleable knowledge-management services. This makes it easy to set up departmental solutions with the Microsoft BackOffice platform, and you can extend or connect them later to enterprise-integrated solutions.

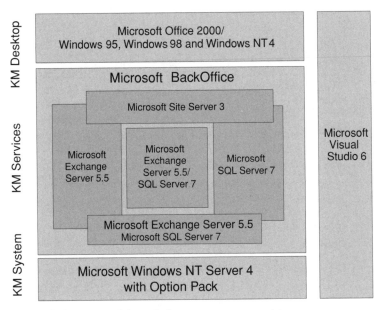

Figure A-3. *Microsoft knowledge-management architecture.*

Basic Conditions for KM

Two conditions must be met to successfully implement a knowledge-management system:

■ Knowledge workers must be prepared to work with technology and to document their work.

■ Knowledge-management systems must support an easy way to create, store, and retrieve information from those workers.

The success of a knowledge-management system depends on the culture of a company supporting the efforts of its people to produce information that can be used to improve the business. Empowered staff producing high-value content will get more use and benefit from a knowledge-management system than will people in companies that don't support sharing of information and ideas in an open fashion. This benefit is even greater for those companies that have expensive human resources or that operate in industries that depend on sharing and reusing information. Chapter 2, "Organizational Barriers," describes ways to help your company overcome cultural barriers such as these. The chances of finding a knowledge-management system (or candidates for a potential one) are extremely high in the following types of companies:

■ Companies with huge R&D efforts (such as those in the computer industry)

■ Companies with big engineering departments (such as manufacturers)

■ Companies that rely on documentation (such as those in the pharmaceutical and medical industries)

■ Technology consulting companies, software-engineering companies, ISVs

■ Accounting and consulting firms

Knowledge-management infrastructures also need to support the capturing of undocumented information (human thought), the sharing of ideas and documents, and the efficient finding of this information (quickly and, more importantly, accurately). This is the foundation of a knowledge-management system that helps to handle information and transfer it into knowledge.

Another characteristic of a system that supports knowledge-management efforts is the existence of a set of common tools used and well known by all users of the system. Tools that provide an entry point to this system either present information or control all interaction with the system. They therefore must be capable of handling all the information that is part of the environment of the knowledge worker. In the best case, only one tool or application should exist for this interface.

MESSAGING AND COLLABORATION

The entry point to all information and applications in a knowledge-management system is also called a *portal* (see Figure A-4). If the environment also supports creating content, it's a knowledge-management desktop. Web browsers, which can present all kinds of information in a rich way, are ideal candidates for such functionality. Portal Services are covered within the "Portals and Search" section, which focuses on content creation, sharing, and collaboration.

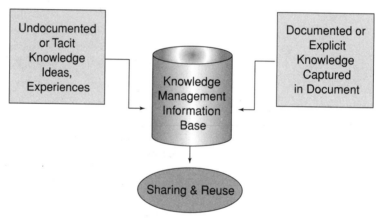

Figure A-4. *Sharing information.*

The goal of the messaging and collaboration module is to create a basic, collaborative knowledge-management system that supports sharing and reusing information. To support the requirement of capturing undocumented knowledge, the Messaging and Collaboration module is a perfect tool. If writing e-mail, sending documents, or participating in discussions are easy tasks for knowledge workers, the motivation to act with knowledge management in mind is much higher than in infrastructures that don't support this or that make it hard to use collaborative features. In a well-designed collaborative environment, this knowledge flow can be easily captured in e-mail, stored in document and discussion databases, and archived in the knowledge-management system for later reuse.

Technology Requirements

The following list describes the technology requirements for messaging and collaboration at each layer: desktop, services, and system:

Desktop
- Easy-to-use productivity suites integrated in all other desktop services
- Comfortable e-mail systems that support collaborative services such as shared calendars, task lists, contact lists, and team-based discussions
- Web browser for browsing and presenting the documents to the user
- Simple search functionalities such as file services integrated with the operating system or search services integrated with an application (e-mail, discussions)

Services
- Collaboration services with a multi-purpose database for capturing the collaborative data
- Web services for providing the access layer to documented knowledge
- Indexing services for full-text search of documents

System
- Well-organized central-storage locations such as file, Web servers, and document databases

Microsoft Technologies

Figure A-5 shows the three knowledge-management platform layers—system, services, and desktop—configured for messaging and collaboration. The following list is an overview of the functions of each part:

- **Microsoft Office and Microsoft Outlook** Helps you build the basic front-end for the end-users of the knowledge-management system for creating, capturing, and organizing their information sources for effective working. For knowledge-management services, Microsoft Windows and Microsoft Office provide basic search services for documents, while the Microsoft Outlook search services find information in e-mail and discussion threads.

- **Microsoft Internet Explorer** Provides easy access and browsing for all kinds of information. Internet Explorer integrates with Microsoft Office and also allows access to all Microsoft Office documents.

- **Microsoft Windows NT Server** Stores documents in its Secure File Server.

- **Microsoft Exchange Server** Adds e-mail, collaboration, discussion, and document-management features.

- **Microsoft Internet Information Server (IIS) with Microsoft Index Server** Provides basic search and access of documents in file systems over standard Internet protocols.

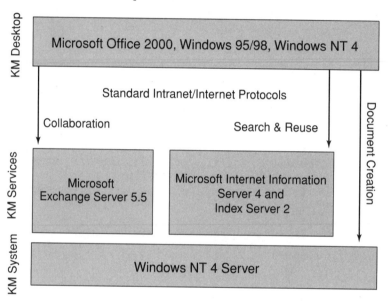

Figure A-5. *Microsoft integration in a collaborative environment.*

The technology enablers in this module are sophisticated e-mail and Web services. Both services must be extensible and customizable to work with the index services in Index Server (for full-text search) or discussion services in Exchange and Office 2000 (for threaded or inline discussions). Equally important are the interfaces with the desktop productivity suite to deliver the collaborative scenario. The following list describes how these Microsoft products satisfy the requirements you learned about in the previous section:

Knowledge Creation and Collaboration (Rich E-Mail, Shared Calendar, Tasks, Contacts, Journals)

- **Office 2000** E-mail, send or store rich Office documents (Access data pages, for example); share common contacts and team calendars; activity tracking in journals.

- **Microsoft Windows 95, Microsoft Windows 98, Microsoft Windows NT Workstation**   Access to heterogeneous knowledge documents with integrated Microsoft Internet Explorer.

- **Microsoft Exchange Server**   Access to knowledge documents with standard Internet protocols like IMAP/NNTP/HTTP or via MAPI (Microsoft Outlook client).

Basic Knowledge Find Services

- **Office 2000**   Exchange database search (threaded discussions, e-mail) with Outlook 2000; possibility to save regular searches in Exchange Public Folder for later reuse.

- **Microsoft Windows 95, Microsoft Windows 98, Microsoft Windows NT Workstation**   File based document search; possibility to save regular searches on knowledge-management desktop or include links to those in Web pages.

- **Microsoft Windows NT Server**   Microsoft Index Server for full text search of documents on file servers.

- **Microsoft Exchange Server**   Rich Views (grouping, sorting, filtering) on Exchange Public Folders.

Knowledge Storage

- **Office 2000**   E-mail and posts to Exchange database (Exchange Public Folders) for later reuse; save to central file server location.

- **Microsoft Windows NT Server**   Secure file server services and Microsoft Internet Information Server for accessing the stored documents over standard Internet protocols.

- **Microsoft Exchange Server**   Multi-purpose database for storing e-mail, news posts, Office documents.

Scenarios and Recommendations

Use Web technologies to access information. One goal of a knowledge-management system is to build a single interface for its users, where as much information as possible is accessible. To achieve that single interface, use Web technologies, especially HTTP and HTML to present information. This will give the most flexibility when accessing data from the knowledge-management desktop. Related recommendations include:

- Use Internet Information Server and HTTP as the primary application-level protocol to hide the document store (file system).

- Use Index Server for full-text search of the documents stored on file servers. Customize Index Server to search different document partitions to reflect the scope of the company's information.

- Use Internet Explorer as an information broker.

Use the e-mail client and integrate it with the productivity suite. The e-mail client with collaborative features (such as calendaring, task management, and discussion threads) is one of the first applications with which users familiarize themselves. Integrate the productivity suite into this application to build a single interface for accessing collaborative information and creating documents. Train users to utilize the Microsoft Outlook messaging and collaboration client out-of-the box integration into the Microsoft Office suite as the primary entry point for collaborative data and corporate document manipulations.

Use the collaboration server to store knowledge assets. With rich, e-mail services integrated with the productivity suite among knowledge workers, the databases on collaboration servers are an important knowledge source. Build a business-related strategy for deploying Microsoft Exchange Public Folders to store discussions and collaborative documents. Enable key Public Folders for e-mail to enhance the support of the knowledge assets captured by Office 2000.

COMPLETE INTRANET

The goal of a complete intranet is to enable knowledge workers to find the right information to solve problems or drive decisions. This core module of knowledge management is supported by a well-organized information network that drives decision making or provides access to all the relevant data needed to get a job done. These decisions must be made quickly enough to get or maintain a competitive advantage. A collaborative environment must be extended if it is to meet these requirements because otherwise it is still too hard for its users to access accurate information, gather all the relevant information, and find hints to other knowledge sources.

A knowledge librarian and an appropriate infrastructure are keys to success:

- From an organizational perspective, there must be a role that knows which organizational group or team needs what kind of knowledge, where information inside and outside a company is located, and how to group and link information together.

■ From an infrastructure perspective, services are needed that support the core characteristics of intranets, such as presenting related information in the form of pointers and links to Web resources, creating and accessing knowledge assets over standard Internet protocols, presenting the right information (groups) to the right people.

The knowledge architect (KA) is introduced during the transition to a complete intranet. The role of the KA is to own the technical and political overview of the information infrastructure of the organization. This role negotiates between groups and handles overlapping competencies and border issues so as to optimize the information-gathering process. The primary task is to survey what's needed to build a successful information network (one that achieves an optimized process for solving problems, driving decisions, and getting a competitive advantage). There can be several knowledge architects who divide the responsibilities for the information services in an organization. In that case, another role might exist, the chief knowledge officer (CKO) that is responsible for coordinating the KAs.

Technology Requirements

The following list describes the technologies required for a successful intranet:

■ Uniform Resource Locator (URL) technologies to link related information together into an information Web.

■ Directory Services that store information about people's roles and responsibilities in the organization.

■ File servers extended with Web servers to access the documents over standard Internet protocols.

■ Home pages on the Web servers for each specific business problem, presenting groups of related knowledge assets.

Microsoft Technologies

The following list describes the Microsoft technologies that help you build a complete intranet:

■ **Microsoft FrontPage** For building and managing Webs, especially to link the information together and to create Web server home pages.

- **Microsoft Office 2000 Web Folders and Server Extensions** To enable the storing and accessing of Office 2000 documents on Web servers through HTTP/WebDAV.

- **Microsoft Internet Information Server with Active Server Pages (ASP)** To access roles and responsibility data in directory services.

- **Microsoft Exchange Server** For a global corporate directory service with information about roles and responsibilities.

- **Microsoft Visual Studio** For developing easy access to directory data, enabling the finding of people, and including this information within Web server home pages.

The main difference in technologies (shown in Figure A-6) over the collaborative environment is the need to define how the documents should be grouped and then to link them together into the information Web. Microsoft FrontPage is the tool for creating and managing the Web groups (Sub Webs) and hyperlinks.

The integration of data from data stores and structures other than file-based documents is more complex than creating and managing a Web with standard HTML and URL technologies. FrontPage, a tool for creating and managing Web sites, delivers some support for developing ASPs and integrating data access. However, Visual InterDev, a Web development system that is part of Visual Studio, allows more flexibility. The application services of both Windows NT Server and IIS, especially ASPs and COM technology, allow the use of most common data sources over the information Web.

Data-access components for these services already exist in Exchange, and they make it easy to access data in Exchange Public Folders or Exchange Directory Service.

Scenarios and Recommendations

Extend the document locations on file servers with standard Internet technologies such as Web services. This tactic will make every knowledge asset stored on these servers accessible from standard Web browsers (through the use of HTTP). It will also streamline the variety of access methods, making it easier for the knowledge workers. Combining that with Office 2000 Web Folders and Server extensions will enable the knowledge workers to store all Office documents direct on Web servers. An interesting effect of the Microsoft Office 2000 Server Extensions is that they enable discussion threads and inline discussions on Office documents stored in the Web folders. This is an additional functionality for knowledge management in pinning additional information, such as comments or suggestions, to the documents to which they relate.

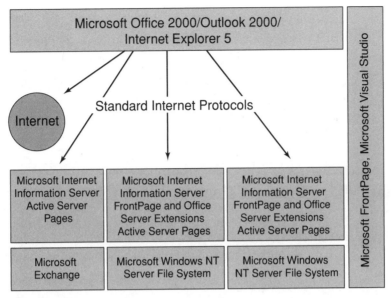

Figure A-6. *The complete intranet.*

- *Build home pages for related information and information groups.* HTML pages should include links to all knowledge sources: not only internal documents but also people and external pages. This will supply your knowledge workers with one-stop access to those related knowledge assets.

- *Use Microsoft FrontPage 2000 for creating HTML pages.* FrontPage 2000 has a variety of collaborative abilities with Office 2000 and Exchange to make it easy to include heterogeneous links.

- *Extend the Messaging Directory with information about roles and responsibilities.* This will enable workers to search the corporate address book for knowledge contacts. Start using the Exchange Directory Service extensively to build your corporate directory, and include basic information about people skills in it. Also, Microsoft Internet Information Server and ASP technologies make this data available from intranet pages.

- *Use integrated development environments to create, manage, and develop your knowledge-management intranet; in particular, use FrontPage 2000 and Visual InterDev 6 to develop the HTML and ASP pages.* Specifically, the use of Design Time Controls (DTCs) helps to integrate dynamic data. For example, the Exchange DTC enables access to Exchange Public Folder data in ASP pages. Other useful features are templates and themes, which help developers build a consistent look and feel for all the Web pages.

■ *Use the Active Directory Service Interface (ADSI) to access the Exchange directory.* ADSI is the Microsoft strategic API for accessing directory data. This is recommended over native Lightweight Directory Access Protocol (LDAP) APIs.

COMMUNITIES, TEAMS, AND EXPERTS

The two prerequisite technologies of knowledge management put all collaboration and document-based knowledge sources together and enables the knowledge worker to browse through informational objects based on knowledge groups. Communities, teams, and experts add the next level of sharing knowledge and turn it to results.

Teams differ from communities in that teams are task driven, and communities are interest driven. Usually a team works closely together (a workgroup) on the same tasks and goals. In many cases, the information produced by a team is closely held within the team until it has reached a level of completeness where it can be shared—for example, in a review—with a broader audience. Communities are mostly driven by interests in the same area and are more loosely coupled (for example, by subscriptions). The information shared by a community is closely held at the final release. Communities are especially useful for building knowledge to higher levels, often by getting successive levels of input from a wide audience.

This enabling component supports knowledge workers' joining communities by subscribing themselves to subject matter sources. The building of communities and teams is characteristic of this component, whether they are driven by the information in the knowledge management system, are administered by a knowledge management architect, or service themselves.

The role of an expert is to qualify and filter information. Each expert is related to a limited set of subjects. (Nobody can be an expert in everything.) Those subject matter experts (SMEs) can be defined in two ways. The first is by organizational function (as defined by the knowledge architect). The second is as well-known experts in their team or organization who have assumed the status of an SME for contributing high quality information or for reviewing it.

The SME is an important role for anyone working within an intranet related to knowledge management. In traditional intranet solutions, there is little control over who can store or upload information into the intranet. This is not a bad thing, and this often helps to build an extensive information repository. But to maximize the usefulness of the intranet, the information should be filtered ("is this really useful information"), classified ("which type or category of information is this"), and grouped together ("which information correlates to this"). This process is part of the responsibility of the SME.

Communities, teams, and experts also control the process of putting information into the knowledge-management system. Filtering, qualifying, approving, or more complex workflow processes for documents and other electronic data need to be established. In a knowledge-management system, these processes are not strictly based on traditional organizational roles (manager, reviewer, approver, author, and so forth) but more on the SMEs. This can add a great level of flexibility to the knowledge-management system and the automated processes.

One example, especially for the SME-based case, is to add some excitement to the system through the possibility that knowledge workers who have achieved expert status in their subject, can subscribe themselves as SMEs (for example, after passing an online knowledge test) and get included into review or even approval processes.

Together with the collaborative prerequisite that enables the infrastructure with e-mail services, this component empowers the knowledge worker to get information quickly and proactively from a knowledge-management system right on the knowledge-management desktop. The e-mail system notifies groups of people with corresponding skills and interests about new knowledge assets and delivers the information that they need.

Technology Requirements

Technology requirements for communities, teams, and experts include the following:

- Directory and membership services that support community building. This is achieved by grouping people together into expert teams working on the same set of information or having the same needs and interests in specific information.

- Forum services to create workspaces for communities and teams that contain all interest-related data.

- Self-subscription services to specific matters of interest for information delivery and subscribing.

- Services to assign specific knowledge-management roles to knowledge workers.

- Workflow services for automating processes based on roles and SMEs.

- Tracking services that follow team contacts and team activities.

- Monitor services that enable SMEs to filter information.

- Dynamic-distribution lists and automated-subscription services for e-mail.

- E-mail services for automating notification, routing, and simple workflow methods.

- Organization-wide databases that integrate and allow searching for skill data and other HR information to enhance communities and teams.

- Home pages on Web servers for each community, team, or expert to speed up the access to knowledge sources.

Microsoft Technologies

The following list describes the Microsoft technologies that satisfy the requirements for the Communities, Teams, and Experts component:

- **Microsoft Office 2000 Server Extensions** For departmental notification services based on subscriptions to Office documents on Web servers (in Web Folders).

- **Microsoft Outlook 2000 and Microsoft Exchange Server** For team activity tracking.

- **Microsoft Exchange Server** For team-based directory services, building forums and workspaces, assigning roles, notification through e-mail, and collaborative workflow services that are interpersonal and team-based workflow intensive for example, approval services.

- **Microsoft Exchange Server or Microsoft SQL Server** As a database with information about people skills (in order to locate the relevant SMEs).

- **Microsoft Internet Information Services with Active Server Pages (ASP)** To access people-skills databases.

- **Microsoft Visual Studio** For development of easy access to directories, forums, and people skills data, as well as enabling the finding of people who are experts in a specific subject.

- **Microsoft Site Server** For building communities, subscribing to knowledge briefs, and notification.

Scenarios and Recommendations

Build community forums, and allow flexibility to add forums dynamically on demand. Use moderated forums to allow SMEs to filter and control content. Related recommendations include the following:

- Build Exchange public folders for forums and assign moderators to them.

- Use Outlook Web access for accessing forums over HTTP or build forum webs with Visual InterDev 6, the Microsoft Exchange DTC, and CDO to access forum data in Exchange public folders.

- Use the Exchange directory and ASP pages build a subscribing mechanism to forums. Build notification services based on Exchange distribution lists for each forum. When knowledge workers subscribe for notifications, an Exchange contact is generated and added to the forums distribution list.

- Use Site Server 3 to provide full text search on the forums.

A different concept is to build communities based on Site Server 3 knowledge manager and shared briefs. Each shared brief is a collection of knowledge assets based on Site Server search catalogs. The knowledge briefs are defined by SMEs. Site Server 3.0 membership directory is used to build communities. Together with Site Server direct mailer and Internet Information Server SMTP service, notification services can be built for each community.

Build teams and team workspaces, and assign roles to team members to manage the workspace and its knowledge assets. Related recommendations include the following:

- Check whether any of the Outlook Team Folder application templates match the needs of the team workspace.

- Use Exchange public folders for team workspaces and Exchange distribution lists for defining teams. Add roles to members in the distribution lists on the Exchange public folder.

- Within public folders, define an information structure that's useful to the team (with subfolders such as tasks, meetings, and contacts) and create views of public folders that show important data first.

- Use Outlook 2000 Public Folder homepages for each team workspace to link knowledge assets, such as people and applications for the team, with contents in Exchange Public Folders (for example, display SMEs for the team on the public folder home page).

- Use rich controls, such as the Outlook 2000 view control, in the folder home pages to display team data, such as calendars and task lists.

- Use Outlook 2000 activity tracking to support team activities, such as sharing contacts.

Extend directory information from the e-mail system with people skills/HR information (as shown in Figure A-7):

- Extend the corporate directory with basic information about subject matter experts (SMEs) using the Exchange directory service

- Add people-skills data to Exchange public folders, or, if a strong relationship exists in this data. base an HR database on SQL Server

- Use SQL Server data-transformation services to consolidate existing people-skill and other HR information from relational databases in Exchange public folders or in SQL Server databases to create a single access point for the knowledge-management system

- Make this information searchable (either in Exchange public folders or in a SQL Server database) with Site Server

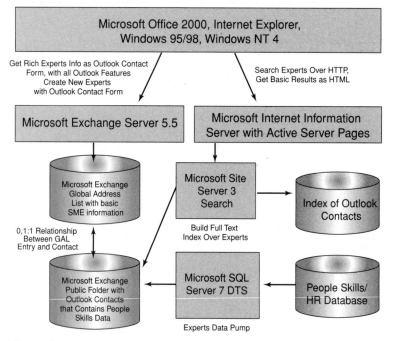

Figure A-7. *Adding expert information to the directory.*

Add notification and routing services to the e-mail system, as shown in Figure A-8. Define roles for approval and simple workflow processes with the messaging directory. Integrate community information in the workflow processes (for example, reviewing and approving documents).

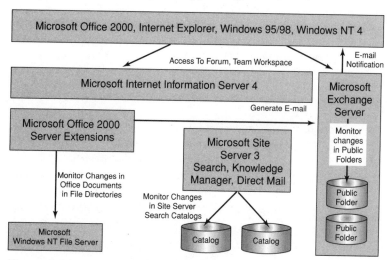

Figure A-8. *Notification and routing services.*

PORTALS AND SEARCH

Almost everybody knows portal services such as Yahoo!, Lycos, Excite, or MSN, where consumer-oriented services allow easy information shopping. Those portals categorize personal interests in groups like news, sports, economy, education, science, entertainment, and so on, and they allow easy browsing within those groups in building a logical hierarchy of subgroups or forums. (See "Communities, Teams, and Experts" earlier in this appendix for more information about forums.) The ability not only to browse but also to search support the consumer in the odyssey to gain knowledge out of the biggest information store on Earth (the Internet). Another huge benefit of these consumer portals is the high customization they provide for its visitors. Objects of interest can be included and placed in a personalized portal, allowing immediate access when visitors return to the portal site.

This technique, when applied to business-oriented goals, is one of the key modules that enable knowledge management—if you follow the idea of the consumer-oriented portals in the corporate world. Business portals provide information to knowledge workers within the company, and they can also quickly supply external suppliers and customers with task-relevant information objects. The goal of such a portal is the transparent enterprise, hiding complexity to facilitate knowledge access over the enterprise information stores with legacy applications. Examples of business portal objects include these:

- Important corporate and team links

- Team-application links

- Incoming mail notification and headers

- Personal tasks

- Corporate search

- Integration of business intelligence data

From the examples, some direct organizational tasks can be defined. Teams in the enterprise need these definitions in order to locate information from inside or outside the company that allows them to include links to that information into the portal. The kinds of data in Management Information Systems (MIS) and/or Enterprise Resource Planning (ERP) need to be in the business portal as well as information on how this data has been made accessible and useful (or intelligent) when presented for analysis.

This component defines also the creation of catalogs that groups related information based on business needs over stores of structured and unstructured enterprise information. This knowledge-management information base allows full-text search against the partitioned data. An extension to the catalogs is the definition of searches against these catalogs by SMEs (see the "Communities, Teams, and Experts" section earlier in this appendix) and makes these search definitions available.

In order to define the catalogs for an organization, there has to be a very good understanding of the business and its processes. At this stage, the knowledge architect needs the support from the different divisions, business units, and departments that understand how their information is organized and how it relates their business goals, tasks, and needs.

Technology Requirements

The following list describes the technological requirements for implementing the Portal and Search component:

- Systems that allow customization of the business portal

- Web browsers with personalization systems offer the ability to include desktop services like e-mail, collaboration data, or business-intelligence tools for accessing rich presentations of MIS/ERP data

■ Development suites for building and maintaining the business portal pages and sites

■ Catalog and search services that integrate all kinds of information sources (for example, file and Web servers, databases, and document -management systems) and crawl-external resources like partner and suppliers sites or the Internet

■ Services to build a virtual single storage location that combines all catalogs for knowledge retrieval

■ Notification services that react to changes in catalogs and integrate with the e-mail system

■ Database replication and transformation services that pull information from different data sources into the search system

Another way to achieve proactive knowledge delivery in portals is through channel technology. The concept of knowledge-management channels is comparable to cable TV channels. The knowledge worker can subscribe to a channel (or get an automatic subscription based on an interest group to which she belongs) that is implemented within an area of the knowledge-management portal. This area is updated each time channel-related information changes in the knowledge-management system. From Microsoft's perspective, the future of this technology is questionable, which may dissuade some users from channel technology. To determine whether your knowledge management solution should include channels, you might consider putting the channel technology through a user-acceptance test phase.

Microsoft Technologies

The following Microsoft technologies are useful for implementing the Portals and Search component:

■ **Microsoft Site Server** For personalizing the knowledge-management portal:

　■ Build catalogs that contain a document index and to integrate data sources (such as file and Web servers, Microsoft Exchange stores, databases, and information captured by crawling Internet sites) into a full text-retrieval system.

　■ Build shared knowledge briefs (searches against Site Server catalogs) and make them accessible on the knowledge-management portal.

- **Microsoft Exchange Server**   For e-mail notification services.

- **Microsoft Office 2000 Web Components and Outlook 2000 View Control**   For building rich portal services that present dynamic data.

- **Microsoft Internet Explorer 5 and Dynamic HTML (DHTML)**   To build sophisticated portal interfaces, hosting rich controls and interaction with knowledge workers.

- **Microsoft FrontPage 2000 and Microsoft Visual InterDev**   To develop and maintain rich portals with components and customized search capability based on catalogs.

- **Microsoft SQL Server with Data Transformation Services (DTS)**   For building a central repository of information related to specific business tasks.

An important quality of a search system designed for knowledge management is that it allows an integrated search of all information sources, even collating and sorting the results. A good practice is to build a central search server that is responsible for delivering the results to the users of the knowledge-management system who get their information (catalogs) from catalog-building servers. Only these catalog-building servers gather the information from the knowledge-base sources, build the catalogs, and propagate these to the search servers. Figure A-9 shows an example.

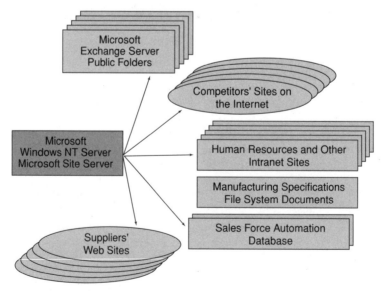

Figure A-9. *A search system implemented with Microsoft technologies.*

Scenarios and Recommendations

Define each content catalog well. This will increase usability of the search function in the knowledge-management system. Related recommendations are in the following list:

■ Too many catalogs will make it difficult to find related knowledge assets later (disjointed result sets). Too few catalogs will result in too generalized content, and it will be difficult to get an exact result set.

■ Building a central data repository (consolidating databases) is preferable to maintaining multiple catalogs in the search topology. Consolidation will simplify the search infrastructure and management.

■ Include collaboration data in Exchange public folders (for example, bulletin boards, forums, and discussion databases) and MIS/ERP data in the catalogs.

■ Replicate Lotus Notes/Lotus Domino databases and applications in Exchange public folders and applications by using Microsoft Lotus Notes Application Connector. The application connector provides bi-directional replication, which allows the sharing of discussion and other databases. The information in the public folders can then be indexed and searched with Site Server.

■ Use SQL Server Data Transformation Services (DTS) to consolidate MIS/ERP data and legacy databases that need to be included in the virtual storage of the knowledge management system.

■ Use the e-mail client as the knowledge management portal. As the e-mail client is the focus of information sharing and is typically one of the first applications a knowledge worker uses in daily business, use it for hosting the portal pages.

■ Use the Outlook Today feature in Outlook 2000 for the portal service and integration with personal productivity data (see Figure A-10). The Outlook 2000 View Control provides great flexibility in integrating collaborative data into the Outlook Today portal page.

■ Make the Outlook Today feature in Outlook 2000 the start page for all users, to guide them to the appropriate knowledge assets depending on their business unit, information, needs, and interests.

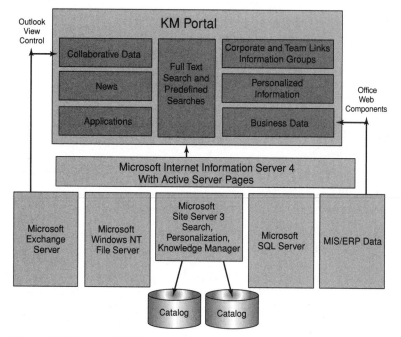

Figure A-10. *Knowledge-management portals with integrated information sources.*

- Include business-intelligence (BI) data in the knowledge-management portal. Speeding up the decision process is one goal of knowledge management, and placing BI data on the portal allows dynamic viewing of data that supports decision making. Use Office 2000 Web Components, such as the Excel 2000 PivotTable component or Access 2000 Data Access Pages, to put business intelligence on the knowledge-management portal.

- Make the knowledge-management portal customizable. This will allow the knowledge workers to optimize the organization of their knowledge-management desktop, thereby applying the knowledge resources they need most and getting better results.

- Use the Site Server personalization system and its active user object to make the knowledge-management portal customizable. Use SQL Server for the personalization directory.

- Use the personalization DTC in Visual InterDev to support the development of customizable portals.

CONTENT MANAGEMENT

The Portals and Search component addresses the problem of searching for knowledge in all information sources in the enterprise. This knowledge includes structured and unstructured internal information objects such as Office documents, collaborative data, MIS and ERP systems, and experts, as well as information from outside sources such as partners, suppliers, and competitors. External sources, and in particular the Internet, represent tremendous potential for gathering knowledge if the criteria for including such information are chosen well. All of the pools of information sources that are part of, and accessible to, the knowledge-management system combine to build the knowledge-management information base.

This component handles how knowledge assets get into the knowledge-management information base. To handle this new complexity of the knowledge management information base and to help the knowledge workers to stay focused on solving business problems (without disappearing in technology), a sophisticated knowledge-management taxonomy needs to be built based on metadata (data that describes other data). The Portals and Search component also needs to publish information in the knowledge base, for example, categories and attributes. The knowledge management information base must then be made accessible through operations driven by the metadata complex. See Figure A-11.

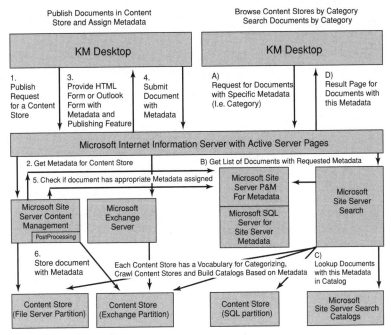

Figure A-11. *Vocabulary based on categories and attributes.*

In the publishing process, several things should be considered concerning the knowledge-management taxonomy. Although tagging documents with metadata is important for the quality of content in this stage of document publishing, it is a burden for people to submit information if tagging the metadata is a complex or time-consuming process. One of the basic conditions mentioned at the beginning of this roadmap was that a knowledge-management system must encourage users to submit information. Positive aspects for promoting this condition are the building of well-focused communities (see "Communities, Teams, and Experts," earlier in this appendix), so users feel part of and respected in a concentrated team and don't lose their inclination or motivation to submit material. Building huge submission and posting systems in which users don't get recognized or rewarded will discourage them from providing their knowledge, which therefore prevents the company from evolving a culture for knowledge management.

Technology Requirements

The following are features that are available for searching external knowledge sources:

- Listing and browsing.

- Sorting.

- Grouping.

- Filtering.

- Searching.

- Publishing information to the knowledge-management information base.

- Finding the right metadata—essential to managing information—is a challenging process for the knowledge manager. Too much metadata will add high complexity to the system, lowering the overall effectiveness, as it becomes difficult to search, browse, and publish accurately.

- Too little metadata will lead to only rough partitions that bring about fuzzy information results.

As you read earlier, the process of publishing new knowledge information is critical for maximizing the quality and usefulness of the knowledge-management information base. Knowledge workers need an easy process to classify knowledge assets based on the defined metadata. SMEs (see "Communities, Teams, and Experts," earlier in this appendix) can be leveraged to support this process of assuring quality and are of great importance to this module. Their task is the final classification, filtering, and approval of the published knowledge assets. One solution is to provide pre-tagging features for all users in a review and approval loop and also to process tags that the SMEs add.

Many of the functionalities required for this component are implemented today in document-management systems. Most of these integrate into BackOffice and should be taken into consideration when building content-management solutions. In the Microsoft environment, there are several options for implementing content-management stores, which are essentially partitions of related information, especially for documents. In the Site Server scenario, content stores are implemented with the NTFS file system.

Microsoft Technologies

The following Microsoft products and technologies are available for implementing content management in your knowledge-management solution:

- NTFS file system
- Microsoft Exchange
- Microsoft SQL Server

Using the available technologies, knowledge-management functionality can be implemented as shown in the following list, which also summarizes the criteria used when deciding on the appropriate content store for a specific solution:

File System with Site Server 3.0

- **Publishing Based on Metadata: Strong**   Site Server content management
- **Rich Views Based on Metadata: Weak**   Site Server P&M and Knowledge Manager
- **Subscription and Notification Services: Medium**   Site Server Knowledge Manager
- **Approval and Workflow Processes: Weak**   Site Server content management

Exchange Server

- **Publishing Based on Metadata: Strong**   Outlook or HTML forms

- **Rich Views Based on Metadata: Awesome**   Built-in views, sorting, grouping, filtering

- **Subscription and Notification Services: Strong**   Out-of-the box features, such as Public Folder rules; list server functionalities *or* integration with Site Server Search and Knowledge Manager

- **Approval and Workflow Processes: Medium**   Collaborative workflow processes; out-of-the box moderated folders; development: Event Scripting for Approval Services; Routing Objects for role-based workflow

- **Check In/Check Out Mechanism: Medium**   Possible without big development work; third-party solutions

- **Versioning Mechanism: Weak**   Possible, but development necessary; third-party solutions

SQL Server

- **Publishing Based on Metadata: Weak**   To develop: application for implementing hybrid model (metadata in SQL Server and documents in file system); third-party solutions

- **Rich Views Based on Metadata: Strong**   To develop: dependent on database design and application development; third-party solutions

- **Subscription and Notification Services: Strong**   To develop: stored procedures and Exchange integration for notification services; application for subscriptions based on SQL tables *or* integration with Site Server Search and Knowledge Manager

- **Approval and Workflow Processes: Awesome**   To develop: great for transaction-oriented work-item processing; most flexible for organizational related workflow solutions, but needs intensive development work; third-party solutions.

- **Check In/Check Out Mechanism: Medium**   To develop: application development; third-party solutions

- **Versioning Mechanism: Weak**   To develop: third-party solutions

All metadata is defined in the Site Server personalization directory. In order to establish a publishing process, content stores are defined in Site Server, and then the created metadata is assigned to a specific content store. Site Server can automatically create HTML forms with metadata list boxes for uploading documents to the content store and can also include the metadata in the publishing process.

These HTML forms can be customized with FrontPage 2000 or Visual InterDev. Site Server supports the creation of content stores for the NTFS file system only.

Through the use of Exchange as a content store, Outlook forms or HTML forms can be created with MAPI-properties as metadata, and the document can then be treated as an attachment to the form. The Exchange Mesa DB Lookup Control can be used to dynamically populate metadata properties on Outlook forms. This scenario can also use the post-processing feature of Site Server to create an Outlook form out of an ASP page with CDO, assign all metadata as MAPI properties, and attach the published document to that Outlook form.

One of the challenges of a knowledge-management system is understanding how the users of the knowledge-management system interact with the knowledge-management information base. The regular analysis of usage and content to ensure that the knowledge-management system fulfills its purpose and is up to date is essential for the success of the system. Unused or useless documents or other information (which might be identified by value scores from readers) should be removed by garbage-collection services from the knowledge-management information base.

Content that is not valuable to users needs to be identified, and content that has great value can be presented in hit lists on the knowledge-management portal or distributed through notification services in e-mail.

An interesting extension is the creation of a hit list that includes information about people. Well-known SMEs who have read a particular document are listed, along with related documents they have read to become experts. A second variation is the possibility for everybody to review and submit comments (or vote how valuable this information was for them) to documents. This list can be shown as an extension of the list of professionals (well-known SMEs) who made comments (for example, "what other people think about that document").

Site Server Analysis supports this task. It has several tools to analyze the usage of the knowledge-management site, including who visits the knowledge-management system, where they go, how long they stay, and so forth. Additionally, Site Server's analysis tools find broken links or outdated content. Site Server has also a voting component that can be used for implementing rating systems in the knowledge-management system.

Scenarios and Recommendations

Define each content class and its associated metadata well. This will increase the usability of the publishing and search functionality of your knowledge-management system. Additional recommendations include the following:

■ Too many content classes will lead to publishing related documents under different content stores, which will make it more difficult to find them later (disjointed result sets). Too few content classes will result in too generalized content, making it difficult to get an exact result set.

- The more precisely the metadata is defined, the easier it is to find information based on different criteria. This is especially important as an SME might search and browse for the same data using different keywords from those a beginner would use.

Define a publishing strategy for documents and integrate it into the knowledge-management system. Ensure that, during the publishing process, users can tag the documents according to the defined metadata:

- If documents reside in Exchange public folders, create Outlook or HTML forms and treat the documents as attachments. Think of storing the metadata in special public folders and using the Mesa DB Lookup Control to populate the metadata properties in the forms.

- If documents reside in content stores based on file systems, use Site Server content-management features. Use Site Server as a metadata directory and SQL Server as a storage repository for the metadata. Use Site Server publishing services for creating publishing forms and posting processes for documents.

Use XML as the markup language for assigning metadata to describe and deliver rich, structured data to the knowledge-management information base and applications:

- Use Office 2000 applications (especially FrontPage), Visual InterDev, and XML Notepad to create or extend XML-based documents and data.

- Use Internet Explorer 5 and an XML parser to process XML-based data.

- Use the Site Server tag tool to apply tags to HTML documents and to categorize them. Site Server Search will use these tags to gather and catalog these documents.

Integrate analysis services in the knowledge-management system. This helps to keep useful data in the knowledge-management information base. Use this data also to personalize the knowledge-management portals. Related recommendations include using the following products:

- Use Site Server 3 analysis for analyzing both the usage and content of the knowledge-management system.

- Use Site Server voting components to track the quality of the knowledge management information

Integrate line-of-business (LOB) data to maximize the completeness of the content stores in the knowledge-management system:

- Integrate SQL Server 7 with Data Transformation Services (DTS) for building a consolidated content store of legacy databases.

- If it is not practical to consolidate data using RDBMS systems, use Microsoft Data Access Components and intranet technologies to integrate dynamic data sources.

- Use ActiveX Data Objects (ADO) as a programming interface for consistent, high-performance access to data. ADO is the single data interface for developing one-to-n-tier client/server and Web-based data-driven solutions.

- Prefer OLE DB as a data access provider to RDBMS and legacy databases.

- Use Remote Data Services (RDS) as client-side services to develop data-centric applications within ActiveX-enabled browsers. RDS brings the advantages of client-side caching of data results, update-able data, and support for data-aware ActiveX controls.

- Use Collaborative Data Objects (CDO) for access to Exchange folders and for e-mail functionality. Choose CDO over Messaging API (MAPI) whenever possible, as CDO is the strategic API for accessing Microsoft Exchange data.

REAL-TIME COLLABORATION

Knowledge on a specific subject is often undocumented and is therefore unavailable to most of the organization. This scenario shows some ways of getting the knowledge into a state where an IT system can manage it. This especially focuses on areas where computers can help your workers exchange thoughts, documents, and other aids for capturing this tacit knowledge for the knowledge-management information base.

The process of capturing tacit knowledge can start with the introduction of simple computer-based chat services. Regular meetings arranged with expert groups to talk about specific topics can be extended with these services, well known from the Internet and enriched by building automatic transcripts for the chat sessions. Transcripts can be easily enriched with corporate metadata and stored in the information base for later search and retrieval.

More complex services, such as video conferencing, follow the same concept. The video stream is recorded on video equipment and later transferred to the knowledge-management system. Descriptions and metadata are either merged with this video stream or can stored in parallel in a file or a database. In cultures where such virtual meetings are common, an event database is typically built where upcoming and past meetings are stored together with event titles and descriptions. They are listed or searchable by subject matter (or, of course, by using the metadata), and a hyperlink is provided so that users can join a virtual meeting. If the meeting takes place in the future, integration into the e-mail system ensures that this event is marked in the calendar, and, on the event date, a reminder automatically points the participant toward the virtual meeting. After the event or meeting, on-demand services will make that knowledge available by providing the recorded video out of the knowledge-management information base to the knowledge-management desktop.

When integrating this technology into the scenario of automated knowledge-management services, notifications are sent automatically to the appropriate knowledge workers to remind them of an interesting meeting or event. The appropriate URLs can also be listed on the knowledge-management portal.

An interesting hybrid of both technologies above (chat and video services) is the integration of presentation techniques. In that case, an online presentation that consists of slides is sent over the network. The audience receives the video, audio, and slides of the presentation on its knowledge-management desktop. The chat service is integrated as a separate area on the knowledge-management desktop, and it enables the audience to type questions during the meeting into the chat area. These questions are transferred to the presenter or a person controlling the online presentation. On receiving the questions, the presenter can answer them during or at the end of the event. All three sources—the slides as a static document, the chat as a transcript document, and the audio and video as a stream—are linked together and stored in the knowledge-management system.

The same technologies not only make virtual events available for the knowledge-management information base, but also data from events such as conferences can be captured. Each session on a conference can be recorded and made available for all employees in the events system on the corporate network. Another solution is to produce CDs of the sessions and distribute them to all subsidiaries or make them available for ordering by interested employees.

Real-time collaboration supports sharing the creation process, making it possible for knowledge workers separated by distance to share a single virtual working space and work together to create documents. This includes sharing the creation process using not only a productivity suite but also whiteboard functionality. This kind of technology is also called screen sharing.

Technology Requirements

Technologies that you should use to implement the real-time collaboration component include the following:

- Chat services with transcript functionality for distance discussion

- Video conferencing for virtual meetings

- Screen-sharing services for sharing the document-creation process, using virtual whiteboards, and sharing applications

- Streaming-media services for recording virtual meetings and video (meeting) on demand services

- Event and meeting databases for organizing the virtual event center

Microsoft Technologies

The following list describes the Microsoft technologies that meet the requirements in the previous section (see Figure A-12 for more information about how these technologies interact):

- **Microsoft Exchange Server Chat Services** For chat services and transcripts.

- **Microsoft PowerPoint** For presentation broadcasts.

- **Microsoft NetMeeting** For video conferencing, document sharing, application services, and whiteboard functionality.

- **Microsoft Windows Media Player** For accessing all kind of audio and video streams.

- **Microsoft NetShow Server and NetShow Content Editing Tools** For recording, broadcasting, and multicasting of online events and tagging the content with metadata for linking it to the knowledge-management information base.

- **Microsoft Outlook 2000** For integration with the NetMeeting conferencing software and Microsoft NetShow services.

- **Microsoft SQL Server** For building the events database.

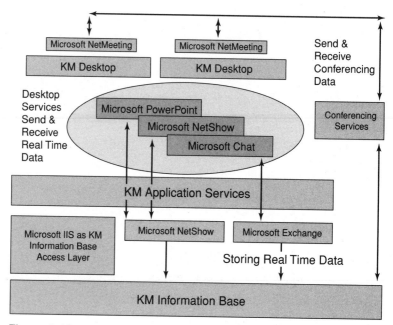

Figure A-12. *Real-time collaboration using Microsoft technologies.*

BUSINESS CHALLENGES

Implementing a knowledge-management solution presents many challenges, such as the following:

- **Complete Integration of Knowledge** How knowledge is built, located, and related to maximize the spectrum of the knowledge management system? (Make knowledge and services from all units within the enterprise accessible.)

- **Technical Integration** What are the infrastructures that need to be in the enterprise knowledge-management system?

- **Central Manageability** What technologies are used for knowledge management in the enterprise and where are the connection or integration points to make the system manageable for a central IT department.

After identifying the knowledge-management services that need to be implemented to improve specific business processes, the technology necessary to support these goals is evaluated. This can be a complex procedure; a summary of system or infrastructure requirements, measured against the services the knowledge-management system should provide, will help to adjust the scope of the project appropriately. Figures A-13 and A-14 show one example of how to develop such a summary by looking at the evolving technology and knowledge-management services from two principle perspectives:

- **Graph of evolving technology and knowledge management over time** This can be built from a feature list that provides functionalities that need to be added over time to improve the services of a knowledge management system.

- **Graph of technology and its effectiveness** This will show, at a high level, how a specific technology added to the knowledge-management system will improve the system's effectiveness.

The two graphs help to determine what level of technology and infrastructure needs to be implemented and the outcomes to be expected from this approach.

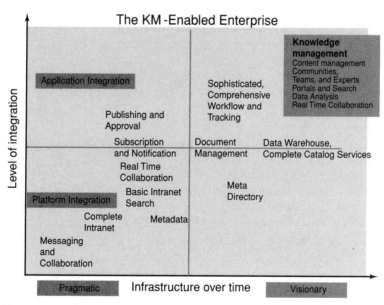

Figure A-13. *Graph of evolving technology and knowledge management over time.*

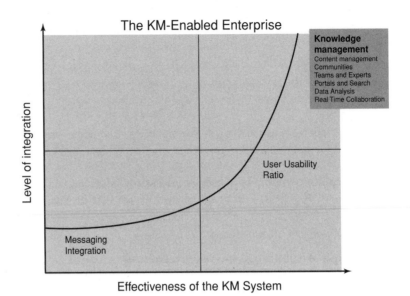

The KM-Enabled Enterprise

Figure A-14. *Graph of technology and its effectiveness.*

One way to tackle the enterprise knowledge-management challenge is by taking a bottom-up approach to building intranets or departmental solutions. In this approach, small pilots are built that implement some functionalities of the components that enable knowledge management. To keep these pilots at a manageable size, they should be locally controlled and include the information needs of a specific department that's not widely scattered throughout the enterprise.

After the start of the pilots, the big picture should never be lost when combining information fragments into an enterprise knowledge-management system. Choose the right technologies, and hire vendors that can deliver a sophisticated solution as well as the interfaces and scalability an organization needs to bind its existing and new information infrastructure and services together.

After the knowledge-management pilots have been deployed, the concepts behind the central junction point for all knowledge-management pieces should be proven. This hub must integrate the pilot systems that were just built. It is the first step in extending the information infrastructure to a centralized, controllable knowledge-management system.

An enterprise knowledge-management system builds, on the back end, an equivalent to the knowledge-management portal for the user. As the knowledge-management portal concentrates all information that is valuable to a specific knowledge worker, the central knowledge-management backbone concentrates all information that is valuable to the whole enterprise. After all knowledge-management islands are built and integrated, this backbone will be the entry point for all enterprise-related information. In terms of knowledge management, this central knowledge-management hub, or knowledge-management backbone, is also called a *metaserver*.

WRAP UP

Requirements for an enterprise-wide knowledge-management system include the following:

- A chief knowledge officer or knowledge architect has been identified and given responsibility for the political, strategic, and technical implementation of knowledge management in the enterprise.

- Culture for technology usage is set up (electronic publishing, collaboration, virtual meetings, and so on).

- All knowledge-management islands are well connected (intranets or departmental solutions).

- Collaborative processes are established (workflow, approval, and information tracking).

- Enterprise knowledge-management information base is hyperlinked.

- Processes keep the enterprise knowledge-management information base healthy.

Glossary

Active Directory   The directory service included with Microsoft Windows 2000 Server. Active Directory stores information about objects on a network and makes this information available to users and network administrators. This service gives network users access to permitted resources anywhere on the network using a single logon process. It provides network administrators with an intuitive hierarchical view of the network and a single point of administration for all network objects.

administrator   A user of a computer running Windows 2000 who has permission to configure that computer and to specify the types of access other users will have to that computer. This type of administrator is also called a local administrator. A network administrator, on the other hand, is a person who has permission to configure a network domain and to specify the types of access other users will have to the resources on that domain.

asynchronous communication   A form of data transmission in which information is sent and received at irregular intervals, one character at a time. Because data is received at irregular intervals, the receiver must be signaled when the data bits of a character begin and end. This is typically done by means of start and stop bits.

authentication   The process by which a system validates a user's logon information. A user's name and password are compared against an authorized list. If the system detects a match, access is granted to the extent specified in the permissions list for that user. When a user logs on with an account on a computer running Microsoft Windows 2000 Professional, the authentication is performed by the workstation. When a user logs on with an account on a Microsoft Windows 2000 Server domain, authentication may be performed by any server of that domain.

Auto PC   A wireless PC for automobiles that provides access to e-mail, voice mail, phone calls, navigation, and other related features. The user interface is voice activated so that a driver can keep with both hands on the wheel.

automated waste The result of spending large sums of money on expensive systems that support inefficient processes rather than building digital systems to support more efficient processes.

bandwidth In communication, the difference between the highest and lowest frequencies in a given range. For example, a telephone line accommodates a bandwidth of 3000 Hz, the difference between the lowest (300 Hz) and the highest (3300 Hz) frequencies it can carry. In computer networks, greater bandwidth indicates faster data-transfer capability and is expressed in bits per second (bps).

batch, batch systems Processes that store transactions in batches to be processed at a later time. Online-transaction systems are replacing batch-processing systems so that businesses see results quicker.

Bluetooth A standard for connecting wireless devices using the 2.45 GHz frequency. Its primary purpose is for short-range communication (10 meters or less) at low speeds (1 Mbps or less). Companies such as Intel are supporting Bluetooth, and this standard for wireless communication is drawing significant attention from the wireless industry.

broadband Network technologies with significantly more bandwidth than the popular standard. The term broadband loosely applies to any high-speed, high-capacity technology.

client A network-connected computer that accesses resources on another network-connected computer, called a server. Dumb clients provide limited capabilities, and an example of a dumb client is a terminal. Smart clients, such as personal computers, support work on the local computer.

Component Object Model (COM) A specification that defines how to build reusable components that can be assembled into new programs or added to existing programs. COM enables componentization of software.

corporate memory A business' intellectual or knowledge assets, which include recorded information and the information in employees' heads.

data A set of unstructured, discrete facts about events and the world. Most businesses capture significant amounts of data in highly structured databases. Businesses analyze, synthesize, and then transform data into information and knowledge.

data mart A small version of a data warehouse containing data that is likely to be used only by the targeted audience.

data mining The process of digging for useful information in databases using advanced tools. The purpose of data mining is to uncover commercially useful patterns and relationships among the data.

data warehouse A database that contains all of a company's information. Data warehouses can exist across multiple databases and multiple computers, and they can include information from different sources in different formats.

dial-up connection Connects you to your network if you are using a device that uses the telephone network. These devices include modems with standard phone lines, ISDN cards with high-speed ISDN lines, or X.25 networks. If you are a typical user, you might have one or two dial-up connections, perhaps to the Internet and to your corporate network. In a more complex server situation, multiple network-modem connections might be used to implement advanced routing.

directory service Both the directory-information source and the services making the information available and usable. A directory service enables you to find an object given one or more attributes (such as finding all duplex printers in Building 26).

disintermediation Removing middlemen from business transactions between a consumer products company and the consumer. Disintermediation occurs via digital transactions on the Internet.

distance learning A system for learning in which students use technologies such as broadcast TV or the Internet to communicate with teachers and other students rather than physically attending classes. Most universities offer distance learning programs, and many schools are strictly based on this model.

document management The electronic management of online and hardcopy documents. Document-management systems include optical scanning to convert paper-based documents into electronic form, databases for organizing documents, and search tools for finding documents.

DNS Server In the DNS client-server model, the server containing information about a portion of the DNS database, which makes computer names available to client resolvers seeking name resolution across the network.

domain In Windows 2000, a collection of computers (as defined by the administrator of a Windows 2000 Server network) that share a common directory database. A domain provides access to the centralized user accounts and group accounts maintained by the domain administrator. Each domain has a unique name.

domain controller In a Windows 2000 Server domain, the computer running Windows 2000 Server that manages user access to the network, which includes logging on, authentication, and access to the directory and shared resources.

domain namespace The database structure used by the Domain Name System.

Domain Name System (DNS) A static, hierarchical name service for TCP/IP hosts. The network administrator configures the DNS with a list of host names and IP addresses, allowing users of workstations configured to query the DNS to specify remote systems by host names rather than by IP addresses. For example, a workstation configured to use DNS name resolution could use the command *ping remotehost* rather than *ping 1.2.3.4* if the mapping for the system named remotehost was contained in the DNS database. DNS domains should not be confused with Windows 2000 networking domains.

dynamic-link library (DLL) An operating-system feature that allows executable routines (generally serving a specific function or set of functions) to be stored separately as files with .dll extensions and to be loaded only when needed by the program that calls them.

electronic commerce (e-commerce) Commercial processes that occur digitally over a network such as the Internet. Business-to-business and business-to-consumer transactions on the Internet are examples of e-commerce.

Electronic Data Interchange (EDI) Standards for controlling how businesses transfer documents, including purchase orders and invoices, between computers. EDI eliminates much paperwork for many large businesses, but it is too complex for small and medium businesses. XML will likely replace EDI as the preferred method for transferring the same types of information.

embedded object Information created in an application that has been pasted inside a document created in another application. When information is embedded, you can edit it in the new document using toolbars and menus from the original program. To edit the embedded information, double-click it to make the toolbars and menus from the program used to create the information appear. Embedded information is not linked to the original. If you change information in one place, it is not updated in the other.

Enterprise Resource Planning (ERP) Applications that some companies use to coordinate sales and order information with manufacturing processes. The goal is to more accurately schedule production and reduce inventory.

executive information system (EIS) Tools that organize information into categories and provide reports for senior management. Traditionally, EIS systems were difficult to integrate with other sources of business information. In today's vernacular, EIS stands for enterprise information system and provides similar information to a broader audience within the organization.

explicit knowledge The result of capturing and providing context to experiences and ideas: explicit experiences. Explicit knowledge is usually stored in partially structured content such as documents, e-mail, and voice mail. Businesses manage information to make it easy to find, reuse, and learn.

extensible markup language (XML) A markup language that describes the structure of content. XML provides a mechanism for indexing data for manipulation. XML is an exciting innovation that provides a way for businesses to exchange data over the Internet.

extensible style language (XSL) A style sheet language that defines how to map structured XML data to another source such as HTML. XSL is different from CSS, a standard for defining the appearance of Web pages.

extranet An extension to a company's intranet that connects its suppliers and customers to make those relationships more efficient.

FAT (file allocation table) A table or list maintained by some operating systems to keep track of the status of various segments of disk space used for file storage. The file allocation table is also called the FAT file system or the FAT-16 file system.

FAT32 A derivative of the File Allocation Table file system. FAT32 supports smaller cluster sizes than FAT, which results in more efficient space allocation on FAT32 drives.

fault tolerance Ensures data integrity when hardware failures occur. In disk management, mirrored volumes and RAID-5 volumes are fault tolerant.

feedback loop A continuous cycle of improvement and feedback. Digital processes create feedback loops by enabling customers to provide feedback to the people who need it.

file system In an operating system, the overall structure in which files are named, stored, and organized. NTFS, FAT, and FAT32 are types of file systems.

global group For Windows 2000 Server, a group of user accounts that can be used in its own domain and in trusting domains. In all those places, a global group can be granted rights and permissions and can become a member of local groups. However, a global group can contain user accounts only from its own domain. Global groups provide a way to create sets of users from inside the domain, available for use both in and out of the domain. Global groups cannot be created or maintained on computers running Windows 2000 Professional. However, for computers running Windows 2000 Professional that participate in a domain, domain global groups can be granted rights and permissions at those workstations and can also become members of local groups at those workstations.

group A collection of users, computers, contacts, and other groups. Groups can be used to enforce security or to facilitate e-mail distribution. Distribution groups are used only for e-mail. Security groups are used both to grant access to resources and as e-mail distribution lists.

group account A collection of user accounts. By making a user account a member of a group, you give that user all the rights and permissions granted to the group.

group memberships The groups to which a user account belongs. Permissions and rights granted to a group are also provided to its members. In most cases, the actions a user can perform in Windows 2000 are determined by the group memberships of the user account the user is logged on to.

group name A unique name identifying a local group or a global group to Windows 2000. A group's name cannot be identical to any other group name or user name in its own domain or computer.

groupware Software that enables users to collaborate over the network about a particular product or service. Groupware traditionally includes e-mail, document sharing, scheduling, and document tracking.

handheld Descriptor for lightweight, small computers that provide specific features for mobile users, including calendaring, e-mail, and task lists. A common term for a handheld device is personal digital assistant.

hexadecimal A base-16 number system whose numbers are represented by the digits 0 through 9 and the (uppercase or lowercase) letters A (equivalent to decimal 10) through F (equivalent to decimal 15).

host The primary computer, usually a mainframe, in a system that contains personal computers or terminals.

hub A common connection point for devices in a network. Typically used to connect segments of a local area network (LAN), a hub contains multiple ports. When a packet arrives at one port, it is copied to the other ports so that all segments of the LAN can see all packets.

Hypertext Markup Language (HTML) The markup language that defines how to format documents for viewing in a Web browser or applications such as Microsoft Word 2000. HTML describes how to format text, align paragraphs, present images, format tables, and so on. It also describes which document to load when users click a link.

infrared Light that is beyond red in the color spectrum. Although the light is not visible to the human eye, infrared transmitters and receivers can send and receive infrared signals.

Infrared Data Association (IrDA) The organization of computer, component, and telecommunications vendors who establish the standards for infrared communication between computers and peripheral devices, such as printers.

infrared device A computer, or a computer peripheral such as a printer, that can communicate using infrared light.

infrared port An optical port on a computer used to communicate with other computers or devices using infrared light. Communication is achieved without cables. Infrared ports can be found on some laptops, notebooks, printers, and cameras. An infrared port might also be added to a computer with an infrared dongle (or hardware security device) connected to a PCI card, a serial port, a parallel port (for a printer), or a direct connection to the motherboard.

input/output (I/O) port A channel through which data is transferred between a device and the microprocessor. The port appears to the microprocessor as one or more memory addresses through which it can send or receive data.

Integrated Services Digital Network (ISDN) A type of phone line used to enhance WAN speeds. ISDN lines can transmit at speeds of 64 or 128 kilobits per second, as opposed to standard phone lines, which typically transmit at 56 kilobits per second. An ISDN line must be installed by the phone company at both the server site and the remote site.

Internet Protocol (IP) The messenger protocol of TCP/IP, responsible for addressing and sending TCP packets over the network. IP provides a best-effort, connectionless delivery system that does not guarantee that packets arrive at their destination or that they are received in the sequence in which they were sent.

Internet service provider (ISP) A company that provides individuals or companies access to the Internet and the World Wide Web. When you sign a contract with an ISP, you are provided a telephone number, a user name, a password, and other connection information so you can connect your computer to the ISP's computers. An ISP typically charges a monthly fee and/or hourly connection fees.

interrupt request (IRQ) line Hardware line over which devices can send signals to get the attention of the processor when the device is ready to accept or send information. IRQ lines are numbered from 0 to 15. Each device must have a unique IRQ line.

intranet A network that uses Internet-based technologies but is accessible only by computers and users within the company. Intranets enable digital processes within companies. An intranet might include e-mail, private Web pages, private mailing lists, and so on.

IP address Used to identify a node on a network and to specify routing information. Each node on the network must be assigned a unique 32-bit IP address, which is made up of the network ID plus a unique host ID assigned by the network administrator. This address is typically represented in dotted-decimal notation, with the decimal value of each 8-bit value in the address separated by a period (for example, 138.57.7.27). In Windows 2000, the IP address can be configured statically on the client or configured dynamically through DHCP (Dynamic Host Configuration Protocol).

just-in-time The concept of delivering items and information when needed, not before and not after. With regard to inventory management, just-in-time means that suppliers deliver materials just before manufacturing, reducing inventory and lowering costs.

knowledge Information about employees' experiences, business processes, and so on that suggests effective action.

knowledge worker Employees whose basic job is to analyze information and make decisions based on that information. Digital processes transform employees into knowledge workers by providing better information about their jobs.

Layer 2 Tunneling Protocol (L2TP) An industry-standard Internet tunneling protocol. Unlike Point-to-Point Tunneling Protocol (PPTP), L2TP does not require IP connectivity between the client workstation and the server. L2TP requires only that the tunnel medium provide packet-oriented point-to-point connectivity. The protocol can be used over media such as Asynchronous Transfer Mode (ATM), Frame Relay, and X.25. L2TP provides the same functionality as PPTP. Based on Layer 2 Forwarding and PPTP specifications, L2TP allows clients to set up tunnels across intervening networks.

legacy A term that implies older technology, hardware and software, that companies will replace at some future date. Integrating modern technologies with legacy technology is important for companies until they can replace older systems.

linked object An object that is inserted into a document but still exists in the source file. When information is linked, the new document is updated automatically if the information in the original document changes. If you want to edit the linked information, double-click it. The toolbars and menus from the original program will appear. If the original document is on your computer, changes that you make to the linked information will also appear in the original document.

local area network (LAN) A group of computers and other devices dispersed over a relatively limited area and connected by a communications link that allows any device to interact with any other on the network.

local computer The computer to which you can log on as a user. More specifically, a local computer is a computer that you can access directly without using a communications line or a communications device, such as a network card or a modem. Similarly, running a local program means running the program on your computer, as opposed to running it from a network server.

local group For computers running Windows 2000 Professional and member servers, a group that can be granted permissions and rights on the local computer, and (if the computer participates in a domain) user accounts and global groups both from its own domain and from trusted domains.

local user profiles User profiles that are created automatically on the computer the first time a user logs on to a computer running Windows 2000 Professional or Windows 2000 Server.

mandatory user profile A user profile that is not updated when the user logs off. It is downloaded to the user's desktop each time the user logs on. It is created by an administrator and assigned to one or more users to create consistent or job-specific user profiles. Only members of the Administrators group can change profiles.

metadata Data that describes data. For example, title, subject, and author are pieces of metadata that describe elements of documents.

Microsoft Management Console (MMC) A framework for hosting administrative tools called consoles. A console is defined by the items on its tree, which might include folders or other containers, Web pages, and other administrative items. A console has one or more windows that can provide views of the console tree along with the administrative properties, services, and events that are acted on by the items in the console tree. The main MMC window provides commands and tools for authoring consoles. The authoring features of MMC and the console tree itself might be hidden when a console is in user mode.

middleware Software that translates information between two applications.

mirror A copy of a volume. Each mirror of a volume resides on a different disk. If one mirror becomes unavailable (due to a disk failure, for example), you can use the other mirror to gain access to the volume's data.

mirror set See mirrored volume.

mirrored volume A fault-tolerant volume that duplicates data on a physical disk. It provides data redundancy by using a copy (mirror) of the volume to duplicate the information contained on the volume. The mirror is always located on a different disk. If one of the physical disks fails, the data on the failed disk becomes unavailable, but the system continues to operate using the unaffected disk. A mirrored volume is slower than a RAID-5 volume in read operations but faster in write operations. You can create mirrored volumes only on dynamic disks. In Windows NT 4, a mirrored volume was known as a mirror set.

modem Short for modulator/demodulator, a device that allows computer information to be transmitted and received over a telephone line. The transmitting modem translates digital computer data into analog signals that can be carried on a phone line. The receiving modem translates the analog signals back to digital form.

multihomed computer A system that has multiple network cards or that has been configured with multiple IP addresses for a single network card.

multilink dialing Combines the bandwidth of two or more physical communication links to increase your remote access bandwidth and throughput using Remote Access Service Multilink. Based on the Internet Engineering Task Force (IETF) standard RFC 1717, RAS Multilink lets you combine analog modem paths, ISDN paths, and mixed analog and digital communication links on both client and server computers. This increases your Internet and intranet access speed and decreases the amount of time you need to be connected to a remote computer.

namespace Resources or items that are available to a computer. In MMC (Microsoft Management Console), the namespace is represented by the console tree, which displays all of the snap-ins and resources that are accessible to a console.

natural language processes (NLP) A discipline that combines computer science and linguistics to create hardware and software that can recognize human speech and handwriting.

NetBIOS An application programming interface (API) that can be used by applications on a local area network (LAN). NetBIOS provides applications with a uniform set of commands for requesting the lower-level services required to conduct sessions between nodes on a network and to transmit information back and forth.

NetBIOS Enhanced User Interface (NetBEUI) A network protocol native to Microsoft networking. It is usually used in small, department-sized local area networks of 1 to 200 clients. It can use Token Ring source routing as its only method of routing. It is the Microsoft implementation of the NetBIOS standard.

network administrator A person responsible for planning, configuring, and managing the day-to-day operation of a network. This person might also be referred to as a system administrator.

NTFS (NT file system) An advanced file system designed for use specifically within the Windows NT and Windows 2000 operating systems. NTFS supports file-system recovery, extremely large storage media, long file names, and various features for the POSIX subsystem. It also supports object-oriented applications by treating all files as objects with user-defined and system-defined attributes.

object An entity such as a file, a folder, a shared folder, a printer, or any item in Active Directory described by a distinct, named set of attributes. For example, the attributes of a file object include its name, location, and size; the attributes of an Active Directory User object might include the user's first name, last name, and e-mail address. For OLE and ActiveX, an object can also be any piece of information that can be linked to or embedded into another object.

OLE A way to transfer and share information between applications by pasting the information created in one application into a document created in another application, such as a spreadsheet or a word-processing file.

online analytical processing (OLAP) Databases and processes that can handle more complex queries than traditional relational databases can handle. They provide filtering, advanced calculations, and specialized indexing.

OpenType fonts Outline fonts that are rendered from line and curve commands and can be scaled and rotated. OpenType fonts are easier to read in all sizes and on all output devices supported by Windows 2000. OpenType fonts are an extension of TrueType font technology.

owner In Windows 2000, the person who controls how permissions are set on every file and folder on an NTFS volume and who can grant permissions to others. In the Macintosh environment, an owner is the user responsible for setting permissions for a folder on a server. A Macintosh user who creates a folder on the server automatically becomes the owner of the folder. The owner can transfer ownership to someone else. Each Macintosh-accessible volume on the server also has an owner.

parity Redundant information that is associated with a block of information. In Windows 2000 Server, parity is a calculated value used to reconstruct data after a disk failure. RAID-5 volumes (also known as stripe sets with parity) interleave data and parity intermittently across a set of disks. Within each stripe, the data on one disk is parity data and the data on the other disks is normal data. RAID-5 volumes, therefore, require at least three disks to allow for this

extra parity information The parity portion of each stripe contains the XOR (the Boolean operation called exclusive OR) of the data in that stripe. When a disk fails, Windows 2000 Server uses the parity information in those stripes in conjunction with the data on the good disks to re-create the data on the failed disk.

parity bit In asynchronous communication, an extra bit used in checking for errors as data is transferred within or between computer systems. In modem-to-modem communication, a parity bit is often used to check the accuracy with which each character is transmitted.

password A security measure used to restrict logons to user accounts and access to computer systems and resources. A password is a unique string of characters that must be provided before a logon or an access is authorized. For Windows 2000, a password for a user account can be up to 14 characters and is case-sensitive. With Services for Macintosh, each Macintosh user has a user password to access the Windows 2000 Server. You can also assign each Macintosh-accessible volume a volume password that all users must type to gain access to the volume.

PC Card A removable device, approximately the size of a credit card, that can be plugged into a PCMCIA (Personal Computer Memory Card International Association) slot in a portable computer. PCMCIA devices can include modems, network cards, and hard disks.

Plain Old Telephone Service (POTS) Basic dial-telephone connections to the public switched network, without any added features or functions. POTS is also an acronym for point of termination station or, more simply stated, a basic telephone line.

Plug and Play A set of specifications developed by Intel that allow a computer to automatically detect and configure a device and install the appropriate device drivers.

Point-to-Point Protocol (PPP) A set of industry-standard framing and authentication protocols that is part of Windows 2000 RAS to ensure interoperability with third-party remote access software.

Point-to-Point Tunneling Protocol (PPTP) Network technology that supports multiprotocol virtual private networks (VPNs), enabling remote users to access corporate networks securely across the Internet by dialing into an Internet service provider (ISP) or by connecting directly to the Internet. The Point-to-Point Tunneling Protocol "tunnels," or encapsulates, IP, IPX, or NetBEUI protocols inside of IP packets. This means that users can remotely run applications that are dependent upon particular network protocols.

port A point on your computer to which you can connect devices that pass data in and out of a computer. For example, a printer is typically connected to a parallel port (also known as an LPT port), and a modem is typically connected to a serial port (also known as a COM port).

portal The primary interface, usually a Web site, that users use as a starting point for their daily activities. On the Internet, portals are users' primary starting points, such as MSN or Yahoo!.

protocol A set of rules and conventions for sending and receiving information over a network. These rules govern the content, format, timing, sequencing, and error control of messages exchanged among network devices.

public switched telephone network (PSTN) Standard analog telephone networks, available worldwide.

RADIUS (Remote Authentication Dial-In User Service) A software-based security authentication protocol widely used by Internet service providers on non-Microsoft remote servers. RADIUS is the most popular means of authorizing dial-up and tunneled network users today.

RAID-5 volume A fault-tolerant volume with data and parity striped intermittently across three or more physical disks. Parity is a calculated value that is used to reconstruct data after a disk failure. If a portion of a physical disk fails, you can re-create the data that was on it from the remaining data and parity. In Windows NT 4.0, a RAID-5 volume was known as a striped set with parity.

random access memory (RAM) Memory that can be read from or written to by a computer or other devices. Information stored in RAM is lost when you turn off the computer.

RAS server Any server configured to run the Remote Access Service on Windows NT or Windows 2000.

redundant array of independent disks (RAID) A method used to standardize and categorize fault-tolerant disk systems.

reengineering The process of designing business processes to improve a company's responsiveness to changing climates.

Remote Access Service (RAS) A service that provides remote networking for telecommuters, mobile workers, and system administrators who monitor and manage servers at branch offices. Users with RAS on a computer running Windows 2000 can, from remote locations, access their networks for services such as file and printer sharing, electronic mail, scheduling, and accessing SQL databases.

Request for Comments (RFC) The official documents of the Internet Engineering Task Force (IETF) that specify details for protocols in the TCP/IP family.

resource Generally, any part of a computer system or network (such as a disk, a printer, or memory) that can be allotted to a program or a process while it is running. Also, any of four system components that control how the devices on a computer work. These four system resources are: interrupt request (IRQ) lines, direct memory access (DMA) channels, input/output (I/O) ports, and memory addresses.

roaming user profile A server-based user profile that is downloaded to the local computer when a user logs on and is updated both locally and on the server when the user logs off. A roaming profile is available from the server when logging on to any computer running Microsoft Windows 2000 Professional or Microsoft Windows 2000 Server. When logging on, the user can use the local user profile if it is more current than the copy on the server.

router In the Windows 2000 environment, routers help LANs and WANs achieve interoperability and connectivity and can link LANs that have different network topologies (such as Ethernet and Token Ring). Routers match packet headers to a LAN segment and choose the best path for the packet, optimizing network performance. In the Macintosh environment, routers are necessary for computers on different physical networks to communicate with each other. Routers maintain a map of the physical nodes on a Macintosh network and forward data received from one physical network to other physical networks. Computers running Windows 2000 Server with Services for Macintosh can act as routers, and you can also use third-party routing hardware on a network with Services for Macintosh.

self-healing The capability for hardware and software to detect and repair problems, often before users are even aware that a problem exists. An example of self-healing software is Microsoft Office 2000, which can detect missing or corrupt files and then repair those files automatically. In Windows 2000, Windows File Protection provides self-healing capabilities to the operating system by detecting when critical system files are the wrong version (or corrupt) and replacing them from the original installation source.

serial port A computer port that allows asynchronous transmission of data characters one bit at a time. Also called a communication or COM port.

server A computer that provides shared resources to network users.

service A program, a routine, or a process that performs a specific system function to support other programs, particularly at a low (close to the hardware) level. When services are provided over a network, they can be published in

Active Directory, facilitating service-centric administration and usage. Some examples of Windows 2000 services are Security Accounts Manager Service, File Replication Service, and Routing and Remote Access Service.

Short Messaging Service A service that enables wireless devices to receive brief messages, including e-mail, Web-based content, and so on. These messages are usually limited to 160 characters of information.

small computer system interface (SCSI) A standard high-speed parallel interface defined by the American National Standards Institute (ANSI). A SCSI interface is used for connecting microcomputers to peripheral devices, such as hard disks and printers, and to other computers and local area networks.

Smart Card A device the size and shape of a credit card that enables certificate-based authentication and single sign-on to the enterprise. Smart Cards securely store certificates, public and private keys, passwords, and other types of personal information. To use a Smart Card, you need a Smart Card reader attached to the computer and a PIN (personal identification number) for the Smart Card.

spanned volume A logical volume made up of disk space on more than one physical disk. You can add more space to a spanned volume by extending it at any time. You can create spanned volumes only on dynamic disks. Spanned volumes are not fault tolerant and cannot be mirrored. In Windows NT 4, a spanned volume was known as a volume set.

spooling A process on a server in which documents are stored until a printer is ready to process them. A spooler accepts each document from each client, stores them, and then sends them to a printer when the printer is ready.

stop error An error (also known as a fatal system error) that causes Windows 2000 to stop responding.

striped volume A volume that stores data in stripes on two or more physical disks. Data in a striped volume is allocated alternately and evenly (in stripes) to the disks of the striped volume. You can create striped volumes only on dynamic disks. Striped volumes are not fault tolerant and cannot be mirrored or extended. In Windows NT 4, a striped volume was known as a stripe set.

tacit knowledge The experiences, ideas, insights, values, and judgments of a business' employees. Tacit knowledge is dynamic and can be tapped only through collaboration and communication with the experts who have the knowledge. Tacit knowledge is embedded in employees' experiences and in business processes.

task worker Employees who have a single, repetitive task and little or no autonomy.

Telephony Application Programming Interface (TAPI) An application programming interface (API) used by communication programs to communicate with telephony and network services. Communication programs like HyperTerminal and Phone Dialer use TAPI to dial, answer, and route telephone calls on conventional telephony devices, including PBXs, modems, and fax machines. TAPI 3.0 also provides Internet Protocol (IP) telephony support, which Phone Dialer and other programs use to transmit, route, and control real-time audio and video signals over IP-based networks such as the Internet.

three-tier architecture An architecture that structures network resources in three layers: the presentation layer (client), the business-logic layer, and the data layer. Personal computers usually provide the presentation layer. PC-based servers usually provide the business-logic layer, and a combination of PC-based and non-PC-based servers provide the data layer.

time to market The amount of time required to deliver a product, beginning to end. Knowledge-management systems help reduce time to market by improving collaboration and allowing knowledge workers to better leverage existing corporate knowledge when developing the product.

total cost of ownership (TCO) The sum of expenses that relate to a computer system or network, including purchasing, installing, and upgrading hardware and software, training people, and managing the process. Industry initiatives designed to reduce TCO include self-healing hardware and software and electronic software distribution.

Transmission Control Protocol/Internet Protocol (TCP/IP) A set of networking protocols that connect computers with diverse hardware architectures and various operating systems. TCP/IP includes standards for how computers communicate and conventions for connecting networks and routing traffic.

TrueType fonts Fonts that are scalable and sometimes generated as bitmaps or soft fonts, depending on the capabilities of your printer. TrueType fonts are device-independent and stored as outlines. They can be sized to any height, and they can appear in print exactly as they do on the screen.

trust relationship A link between domains that allows pass-through authentication, in which a trusting domain honors the logon authentications of a trusted domain. With trust relationships, a user who has only one user account in one domain can potentially gain access to the entire network. User accounts and global groups defined in a trusted domain can be given rights and resource permissions in a different trusting domain, even though those accounts aren't in the second trusting domain's directory database.

tunnel A private, secure link over a dial-up connection between a remote user or a host and a private network.

tunnel server A server or a router that establishes a presence on both the dial-in server and the target network. It terminates tunnels on the dial-in server and forwards data streams to the host on the target network.

Type 1 fonts Scalable fonts designed to work with PostScript devices.

Unicode A 16-bit character encoding standard developed by the Unicode Consortium between 1988 and 1991. By using two bytes to represent each character, Unicode enables almost all of the written languages of the world to be represented using a single character set. (By contrast, 8-bit ASCII is not capable of representing all of the combinations of letters and diacritical marks that just the Roman alphabet contains.) Approximately 39,000 of the 65,536 possible Unicode character codes have been assigned to date, 21,000 of them being used for Chinese ideographs. The remaining combinations are open for expansion.

user account A record that consists of all the information that defines a user to Windows 2000. This includes the user name and password required for the user to log on, the groups in which the user account has membership, and the rights and permissions the user has for using the system and accessing its resources. For Windows 2000 Professional and member servers, user accounts are managed with Users and Groups in Control Panel. For Windows 2000 Server domain controllers, user accounts are managed with Microsoft Active Directory Manager.

user name A unique name identifying a user account to Windows 2000. An account's user name must be unique among the other user names and the group names within a domain or workgroup.

user password The password stored in each user's account. Each user generally has a unique password to type when logging on or accessing a server.

user profile A profile that defines the Windows 2000 environment that the system loads when a user logs on. It includes all the user-specific settings in a Windows 2000 environment, such as program shortcuts, screen colors, network connections, printer connections, mouse settings, and window sizes and positions.

virtual private network (VPN) A remote LAN that can be accessed through the Internet using PPTP.

wide area network (WAN) A network that connects geographically separated computers.

Windows DNA Stands for *Windows Distributed Internet Applications* architecture and defines a framework for building scalable, multi-tier business applications that improve information flow throughout an organization.

Wireless Application Protocol (WAP) New Internet protocols for wireless communications that run on top of other network protocols to transmit data. WAP is for wireless, mobile devices and uses the wireless markup language (WML), which is based on XML.

workgroup A group of users who work on a common project and share information on computers that are connected, often over a local area network (LAN).

Index

Q

Qualcomm, 141
query and reporting tools, 88
QueryTable, 105

R

radio sites, 22
Rankis, Norman, 116-17
RDS (Remote Data Services), 195
ReadFile, 124
read-only memory (ROM), 143
Real-Time Collaboration module, 166, 195-98, 198
real-time notification engine, 157
record-level, 53
records, 103, 106
Reilly, Paul, 36, 38
Remote Data Services (RDS), 195
reports
    business, 90
    direct, 81
    improvement, 11
    planning tool, 72-73
    query, 88
    repositories, 43, 64-66
    synchronization, 53
ROM (read-only memory), 143
routers, 39
Routing Objects, 110, 113
runtime, 93

S

sales
    applications, 57
    automation, 60
    breadth accounts, 50
    data, 52, 68, 88
    depth accounts, 50
    distributors, 55
    field sales, 50
    management, 50
    marketing, 57
    medium-sized accounts, 50
    opportunities, 52-54
    outsourcing, 57
    paper-based, 55

sales *continued*
    productivity, 52
    progress, 56
    prospective customers, 94
    records, 51
    representatives, 52, 55, 62, 67, 93
    resellers, 63
    revenue, 52
    schedules, 56
    segmentation, 50
    targets, 94
    telesales, 50, 53
    timesavers, 5, 53
    tracking, 49-50, 52, 113
    turn-around time, 54
    updates, 53, 56
    Web site, 63
sales force, 50-53
    application, 59
    automation, 58, 68, 113
    case study, 148
    collaboration, 55
    distributors, 55
    management, 50
    productivity, 52
    paper-based, 55
    representatives, 55
    resellers, 63
    segmentation, 50
    Snyder, case study, 60-64
    tracking, 49-50, 113
    Web site, 63
SAP HR R/3, 75, 78, 82
SAPI (Speech Application Programming Interface), 158
SAP R/3, 72, 78, 80, 82-83
scalable products, 73, 88, 113, 126-27
Schedule+ 7.5. *See* Microsoft Schedule+ 7.5
Schultz, Eric, 141
Scott, Greg, 114-16
screens, opening, 23
search services, 184-86
secure wireless communications, 148
security methodologies, 128-30
servers
    applicaitons, 108
    ASP, 64
    back-end systems, 60

JERRY HONEYCUTT

Jerry Honeycutt empowers people to work and play better by helping them use popular technologies such as the Microsoft Windows and Microsoft Office product families. In the last several years, he has written 25 books, most available internationally. His most recent book from Microsoft Press is *Introducing Microsoft Windows 2000 Professional.* Jerry is also a frequent speaker at public events and is presenting a Microsoft-sponsored seminar called *Best Practices for Large Scale Distribution of Office 2000 and Windows 2000.* Prior to his career as a writer and speaker, Jerry helped companies such as Southland Corporation, IRM, Nielsen North America, and IBM to build and use technology. Jerry graduated from University of Texas at Dallas in 1992 with a BS degree in Computer Science. Prior to attending UTD, he spent three years at Texas Tech University in Lubbock, Texas. In his spare time, Jerry plays golf, dabbles with photography, and travels.

The manuscript for this book was prepared using Microsoft Word 2000. Pages were composed by ProImage using Adobe PageMaker 6.5, with text in Garamond and display type in Helvetica Black. Composed pages were delivered to the printer as electronic prepress files.

Principal Compositor
ProImage/Jimmie Young

Copy Editor
Anne Owen

Technical Editor
Allen L. Wyatt

Indexer
Bill Meyers

Ready
solutions
for the
IT administrator

Keep your IT systems up and running with the ADMINISTRATOR'S COMPANION series from Microsoft. These expert guides serve as both tutorials and references for critical deployment and maintenance of Microsoft products and technologies. Packed with real-world expertise, hands-on numbered procedures, and handy workarounds, ADMINISTRATOR'S COMPANIONS deliver ready answers for on-the-job results.

Microsoft® SQL Server™ 7.0 Administrator's Companion

U.S.A.	$59.99
U.K.	£38.99 [V.A.T. included]
Canada	$89.99
ISBN	1-57231-815-5

Microsoft Exchange Server 5.5 Administrator's Companion

U.S.A.	$59.99
U.K.	£38.99 [V.A.T. included]
Canada	$89.99
ISBN	0-7356-0646-3

Microsoft Windows® 2000 Server Administrator's Companion

U.S.A.	$69.99
U.K.	£45.99 [V.A.T. included]
Canada	$107.99
ISBN	1-57231-819-8

Microsoft Systems Management Server 2.0 Administrator's Companion

U.S.A.	$59.99
U.K.	£38.99 [V.A.T. included]
Canada	$92.99
ISBN	0-7356-0834-2

mspress.microsoft.com

There's no *substitute* for *experience.*

Now you can apply the best practices from real-world implementations of Microsoft technologies with NOTES FROM THE FIELD. Based on the extensive field experiences of Microsoft Consulting Services, these valuable technical references outline tried-and-tested solutions you can use in your own company, right now.

Deploying Microsoft® Office 2000
(Notes from the Field)
U.S.A. $39.99
U.K.   £25.99 [V.A.T. included]
Canada $59.99
ISBN 0-7356-0727-3

Deploying Microsoft SQL Server™ 7.0
(Notes from the Field)
U.S.A. $39.99
U.K.   £25.99
Canada $59.99
ISBN 0-7356-0726-5

Optimizing Network Traffic
(Notes from the Field)
U.S.A. $39.99
U.K.   £25.99 [V.A.T. included]
Canada $59.99
ISBN 0-7356-0648-X

Managing a Microsoft Windows NT® Network
(Notes from the Field)
U.S.A. $39.99
U.K.   £25.99 [V.A.T. included]
Canada $59.99
ISBN 0-7356-0647-1

Building Enterprise Active Directory™ Services
(Notes from the Field)
U.S.A. $39.99
U.K.   £25.99 [V.A.T. included]
Canada $61.99
ISBN 0-7356-0860-1

***Microsoft*®**
mspress.microsoft.com

Microsoft® Resource Kits— powerhouse resources to minimize costs while maximizing performance

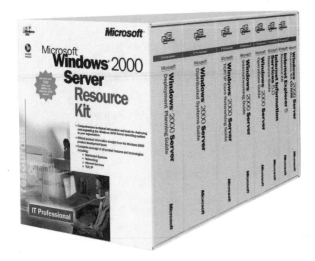

Deploy and support your enterprise business systems using the expertise and tools of those who know the technology best—the Microsoft product groups. Each RESOURCE KIT packs precise technical reference, installation and rollout tactics, planning guides, upgrade strategies, and essential utilities on CD-ROM. They're everything you need to help maximize system performance as you reduce ownership and support costs!

Microsoft® Windows® 2000 Server Resource Kit
ISBN 1-57231-805-8
U.S.A. $299.99
U.K.   £189.99 [V.A.T. included]
Canada $460.99

Microsoft Windows 2000 Professional Resource Kit
ISBN 1-57231-808-2
U.S.A. $69.99
U.K.   £45.99 [V.A.T. included]
Canada $107.99

Microsoft BackOffice® 4.5 Resource Kit
ISBN 0-7356-0583-1
U.S.A. $249.99
U.K.   £161.99 [V.A.T. included]
Canada $374.99

Microsoft Internet Explorer 5 Resource Kit
ISBN 0-7356-0587-4
U.S.A. $59.99
U.K.   £38.99 [V.A.T. included]
Canada $89.99

Microsoft Office 2000 Resource Kit
ISBN 0-7356-0555-6
U.S.A. $59.99
U.K.   £38.99 [V.A.T. included]
Canada $89.99

Microsoft Windows NT® Server 4.0 Resource Kit
ISBN 1-57231-344-7
U.S.A. $149.95
U.K.   £96.99 [V.A.T. included]
Canada $199.95

Microsoft Windows NT Workstation 4.0 Resource Kit
ISBN 1-57231-343-9
U.S.A. $69.95
U.K.   £45.99 [V.A.T. included]
Canada $94.95

Microsoft®

mspress.microsoft.com

For information about Microsoft Press®
products, visit our Web site at
mspress.microsoft.com